MIKE ANDERSON'S
Seafood

Recipes from Mike Anderson's Seafood And Other South Louisiana Favorites

by Michael H. Anderson

Compiled by Angie Perry

Copyright ©1999 by Mike Anderson's Seafood

Illustrations by: Brad Richoux and Jessica Jeffrey

The Mike Anderson's Seafood logo that appears on the cover and throughout this book, was designed by Al Lorio.

First Edition   November 1999   10,000 copies
Second Printing   June 2001   10,000 copies

ISBN 0-9673716-0-0

Printed in the USA by
WIMMER
The Wimmer Companies
Memphis
1-800-548-2537

I am not a professional chef. Neither have I had any formal training in the culinary arts. I am simply a person who enjoys good food and likes to cook. I consider it a blessing to be able to prepare food that people seem to really like and to share it with you, my customers, my friends, and my family. I opened my first restaurant, Mike Anderson's College Town Seafood & Oyster Bar in November of 1975. It was located at 4332 Highland Road (the old College Town Grocery), in Baton Rouge, Louisiana. When we moved to our current location at 1031 W. Lee Drive in Baton Rouge, the name was changed to Mike Anderson's Seafood Restaurant.

My first menu offered four different poboys and oysters on the half shell. There was also a grocery of sorts where fresh and boiled seafood could be purchased. It was my good fortune that the south Baton Rouge community liked what I was doing. As business increased, I began to experiment with the addition of various items to the menu. Among the first additions I made were a seafood gumbo and a shrimp salad. The customers embraced each new dish and growth continued. Mike Anderson's College Town Seafood was becoming a full-service restaurant serving hundreds of people every day. Quite successful for someone with no experience in the restaurant industry.

I started playing football for Louisiana State University the fall of 1967. I was fortunate enough to be named All American my senior year. I never dreamed of opening a restaurant. One of my last endeavors before opening Mike Anderson's College Town Seafood was running a pig farm. Short-lived, but what an experience! Now, after many years of hard work, I find myself with three full-service restaurants. We moved to W. Lee Drive in 1983 and this is where I spend most of my time. We seat greater than 235 people and employ approximately 130 people. In the spring of 1985, the French Quarter location at 215 Bourbon Street, opened in New Orleans. In the years following, I opened locations in two food courts in New Orleans, one at The Riverwalk Mall and one at The New Orleans Center. These locations offer counter service with an abbreviated menu of some of our most popular items. There is also Captain Anderson's, a franchise located in the Holiday Inn in Gonzales, Louisiana. My most recent venture is a full-service restaurant seating 275 people in Metairie, Louisiana.

You know, I have been asked many times over the years to write a cookbook based on the food served in my restaurants. Many of you have asked "Mike, please give me the recipe to the coleslaw dressing." "Mike, what is it that you put in the Guitreau that gives it its color?" Well I guess I put it off as long as I could. I never dreamed when I ventured into the restaurant business those 24 years ago that something I just threw together to satisfy my own taste buds would appeal to so many people. So here it is...my cookbook.

Mike Anderson

I·N·T·R·O·D·U·C·T·I·O·N

To my customers I say, "Thank you." Thank you for coming back time and time again. Thank you for letting me know what I was doing right as well as what didn't quite come together. Thank you for your support over all these years.

I must also thank, in particular, and with love, my family who are my wife, Mary, my son, Michael, and my daughter, Summer. Everything I have worked for has been for you, and I thank you for standing by my side through the good times and the tough times.

Thanks to my mom for all the wonderful home cooked meals while I was growing up. You inspired a love of good food that keeps me cooking.

To my sister, Barbara Cooper, who waited tables in the early days and later worked as a dining room manager and banquet coordinator.

To those who have been with me for many years, especially my assistant, secretary, and friend, Gloria Reaves, who has been with me through it all.—Thank you.

To Harry and Jeanne Robert, Roberto and Mary Sandoval, Gloria Reaves, Debbie Bennett, Richard Picou, Boyd and Beth Perry, Buddy and Carol Shirley, Lynn and Shirley Juban, Bobby Morris, Angie Perry and David Morris who gathered at my home one Saturday night in mid-July to help recall memories of the restaurant and recipes from the beginning.

To Jessica Jeffery and Brad Richoux for their time and efforts that resulted in the wonderful illustrations you see in this book.

To Phan Ngo and Ngoc Phung (Lynn), our husband and wife team in the prep kitchen, thanks for your years of dedication and attention to detail.

To David Morris, my nephew and general manager, who literally got this project off the ground.

To Angie Perry who worked on this cookbook with me day and night until completion.

To all of you I say, "Thank you!"

Finally, I would like to thank all of my managers and employees from past to present who gave their best to make Mike Anderson's Seafood a familiar name in the Deep South.

To all of you who purchased this cookbook or received it as a gift, I hope you enjoy preparing these recipes as much as I have over the years.

DR. HOWARD W. ANDERSON

This book is lovingly dedicated to the memory of my father, Dr. Howard W. Anderson, who, from the beginning, was a source of inspiration. He was always there for me with kind words of wisdom and encouragement and a willingness to do whatever necessary to help, including preparing the payroll week after week in the early days. His greatest gift, though, was just being my dad.

7

T·A·B·L·E O·F C·O·N·T·E·N·T·S

Mike Anderson (signature)

F·O·R·E·W·O·R·D

By Angie Perry

AFTER 25 YEARS THE SECRETS ARE OUT.
WE ARE TELLING ALL.......

I have worked at Mike Anderson's Seafood Restaurant for 3½ years. During this period, I never paid attention to any of the food preparation. While in college, I rarely cooked. After graduating from Louisiana State University in December of 1998, I was approached by the general manager, David Morris, about compiling a cookbook for the restaurant. Having studied advertising and marketing in college, my eyes immediately lit up at the thought of designing a book. I went home and discussed this with my parents and close friends. Two months later, after accepting the job, I found out that there was a tiny catch. Mike Anderson's, of course, a full-service restaurant serving hundreds of customers a day, prepares its recipes in large quantities. This presented a problem for me, the college student with absolutely no cooking skills. After overcoming the obstacles that only a busy kitchen can provide, I learned, and I learned well. In my opinion, I learned from one of the best cooks in South Louisiana.

Every single recipe in this cookbook was reduced to family portions and cooked by Mike Anderson and myself. We cooked recipes to make them absolutely perfect which is our restaurant's standard.

During this time of cooking, testing and tasting, I observed things in the restaurant kitchen that I had never noticed before. You will notice that throughout this cookbook ingredients are listed with the words chopped, fresh, grated, shredded and toasted. The dedicated kitchen employees chop fresh onions, bell peppers, carrots, green onions, heads of lettuce and cabbage every morning. Breadcrumbs are made fresh and the cornbread is made from scratch. Even the lemon juice used in many of our recipes is freshly squeezed. Garlic is minced fresh everyday and Mike Anderson's seasonings and batters are mixed daily as well.

I also found out how important fresh seafood is to Mike Anderson. Only the freshest crawfish and crabs are accepted. Fresh fish are inspected and filleted every morning by trained and dedicated employees. Vegetables are also checked thoroughly, as many of our vendors know, by well-trained employees. Fresh bread is delivered daily. It is still warm to the touch when we open the doors at 11 o'clock.

Good food takes time, as I soon found out. Our gumbo stews for hours, along with many of our other soups. The cheesecakes are cooked at the lowest temperature for hours,

(continued on next page)

just to ensure perfection. Even the stuffed potatoes are made fresh every morning. The kitchen works like clockwork. It is amazing to watch.

The first section of the cookbook "The Basics" is a reference section. This section contains many of the recipes that are a necessity in using this cookbook. After this section, the cookbook follows the layout of the menu. There are "Appetizers," "Fried Seafood," "Specialties," and so on. The last section of the cookbook is unique. This section includes recipes from Mike Anderson's mother, his wife and children, and many of his family, friends and valued customers.

I must admit that it has been fun. I know that my future family will one day be glad that I learned how to cook and cook well. I would like to thank, first of all, Mr. Mike Anderson and his family for giving me the opportunity to work with them on this cookbook.

I would also like to thank David Morris and Gloria Reaves for their long hours of help. To Ngoc (Lynn) Phung, Chi Phung and Phan Ngo, how could we have done this without you!

To Wilbert Zeno, Lester Jones, Amy Zollman and Blair Kornegay, "Thank you."

Thank you to my parents, and a very special "THANK YOU" to my best friend, my mother, Beth H. Perry, who worked daily with me on this project.

This cookbook was written in response to the constant requests from customers, family and friends for Mike Anderson's recipes. After 25 years here they are......

Our Baton Rouge location

1031 West Lee Drive
Baton Rouge, Louisiana 70820

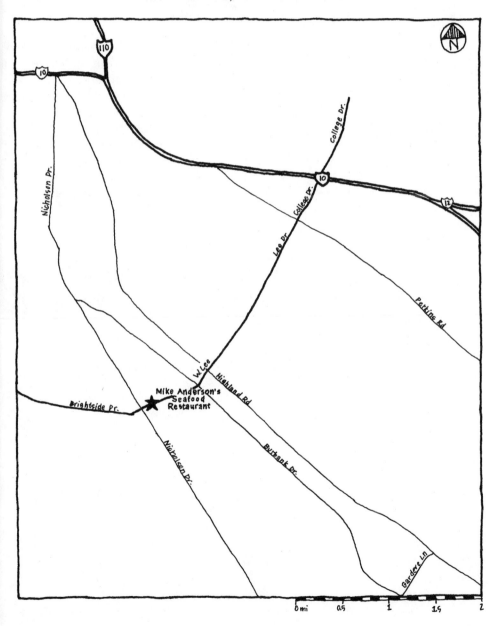

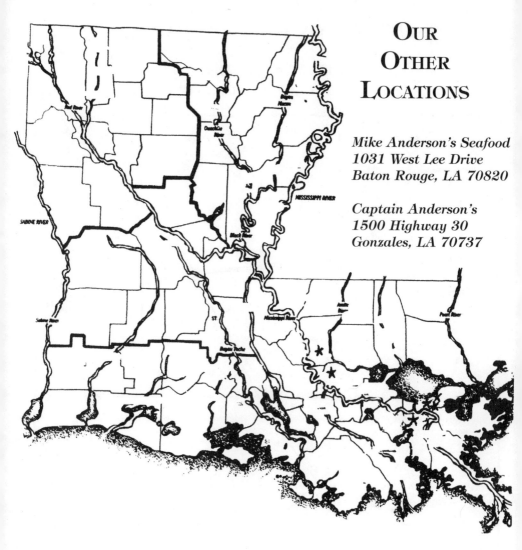

OUR OTHER LOCATIONS

Mike Anderson's Seafood
1031 West Lee Drive
Baton Rouge, LA 70820

Captain Anderson's
1500 Highway 30
Gonzales, LA 70737

Mike Anderson's Seafood
215 Bourbon Street
New Orleans, LA 70130

Mike Anderson's Seafood
2712 N. Arnoult
Metairie, LA 70002

Mike Anderson's Seafood
Riverwalk
1 Poydras St., Suite 163
New Orleans, LA 70130

Mike Anderson's Seafood
New Orleans Center
1400 Poydras St., Number 268
New Orleans, LA 70112

We have a rich history here at Mike Anderson's Seafood Restaurant. As you can imagine, there are stories to be told. This glossary touches on a few of the words, phrases and memories that are a part of our history and have special significance to myself, family, friends, co-workers and maybe even some customers.

ACE
: All you can eat whole catfish. My dad asked me to put this on the menu. We started selling about 10 pounds a week. We now sell about 500 pounds. To my knowledge, the gentleman that holds the record for the most fish eaten was on his 20th fish when I informed him we had run out of fish. We had to increase our order for catfish that week.

Advice
: Many years ago, after a day with lunch sales of only $3.75, my best friend advised me to get out of the restaurant business. My advice.....Don't give up!

Andy
: What many called my father, and sometimes call me.

Archibald
: My father, Dr. Howard W. Anderson, made us all laugh as he recited this joke at our annual Christmas parties. With changes in voice and a variety of gestures he would become the character, Percy, and then Archibald when telling this story year after year. It was a good time.

Bob
: One of my nicknames. This one was acquired after I told friends about one of my favorite episodes of The Newlywed Game.

Cheers
: My waitstaff over the years has been a colorful group. They have always gone the extra mile to make our customers feel welcome. Mary Sandoval and Felicia Leggio made up cheers during football season. These include, "Crawfish Bisque, Étouffée, Come on Tigers, All the Way!" and "Cold Couscous, Hot Boudin, Come on Tigers, Let's Win!"

Crab Boiling
: We all had a lot to learn in the early days. My father once tried to boil crabs in a room with no ventilation. This prevented the water from boiling. I had a restaurant full of people wanting to eat crabs. The line was out the door and the crabs wouldn't boil. Amazingly, people waited for hours to get those crabs.

Elvis
: Another one of my famous nicknames, as in, "Elvis has left the building," code for Mike has left.

(continued)

G·L·O·S·S·A·R·Y O·F M·E·M·O·R·I·E·S

Garlic Bread Served with many of our entrées. Richard Picou, nicknamed "Q", is famous for the night he helped out and just couldn't stop making garlic bread.

Hospital My favorite place to get a haircut. Even if you don't need the haircut, I recommend the head massage.

Host/Hostess The most popular Mike Anderson's Seafood employee when there's a 2 to 3 hour wait.

Howard Yet another nickname, my middle name, my son's middle name and my father's name. "The Howard" (See page 91) was named for my father.

Inflation When I opened College Town Seafood the rent was $200 per month. When I left the Highland Road location, the rent had grown to $8,000 per month. Someone must have been counting the cars in the parking lot.

Knives Important tool in the restaurant business. On the day I opened the restaurant, I realized we didn't have a knife to spread mayo on the poboys we were making. Carol Shirley was called, and quickly came to our rescue, bringing knives from her home.

Liquor License We didn't have one on Highland Road.

"Midnight Hour" My favorite song to sing at past employee Christmas parties. I am also reminded I sang this song after our LSU freshman football team played Ole Miss in 1967.

Mustard Greens Once, my ego inflated by compliments from family and friends, I cooked a pot of mustard greens. I was really impressed with myself when I noticed people going back for seconds, until someone commented that there was 2-inches of mud in the bottom of the pot. My ego deflated, I realized I had a lot to learn (especially about washing mustard greens).

Norman The refrigeration repairman immortalized when he walked into the kitchen while I was searching for a name for the new dish I had just created. Trout Norman and Shrimp Norman (See pages 107 and 108)

Plaster Our location on Highland Road was known for the quaint ambiance created by the falling ceiling plaster. The falling fern baskets were another favorite attraction.

Poboys A traditional south Louisiana sandwich. We once prepared over 100 poboys (roast beef and ham) to be served after the first LSU game of the season, to the hungry fans. As we watched the cars passing by and no one stopped, we started giving them away by means of a quick and calculated toss into the open windows of passing cars. Quite sometime later, a customer revealed that he had been a recipient of one of my "flying poboys."

Poboy Machine   "Jean, Jean the poboy machine" was the nickname given to my sister-in-law, Jeanne Robert, after the many long days she helped out making poboys.

Pots   More commonly found in the attic of College Town Seafood, rather than in the kitchen, to catch the rain.

Pod-Zu   A slang term I picked up years ago that means "my friend." My son, Michael, has been called Pod-Zu by family and friends since he was a youngster. Michael's boat is also named Pod-Zu.

September 13, 1997   The day the restaurant in Baton Rouge caught on fire, destroying the entire kitchen and upstairs offices. We were closed for three months while the kitchen and offices were gutted and rebuilt. The restaurant reopened with a brand new kitchen on December 13, 1997.

Tomatoes   I have used tomatoes many times in my own version of kitchen "dodge ball" or to accentuate and punctuate my instructions.

Upstairs   When the lower level at College Town Seafood would flood, everyone would head for the second level. This encouraged our customers to get to know one another better.

Wooden Menus   While on my honeymoon, in Jamaica, my wife and I dined at a restaurant that used wooden menus. I liked the idea and decided to try it. Employees hand wrote the menus, burned the paper edges, sanded the menu boards, glued the papers to the boards, polyurethaned (3 coats) the boards, drilled and tied the menus together. This was done again and again and again over the years. Customers sometimes take them as souvenirs.

"You Whooooo!"   Buddy Shirley's cry for help one night when he was accidentally locked in the restaurant after everyone had gone home.

"Don't Shoot!"   David Morris's cry to the police when he arrived to free Buddy Shirley the night he was locked in the restaurant. Buddy had triggered the restaurant's alarm and the police had promptly responded to the call. I know Buddy is grateful to David for admitting he recognized him.

1975   The year College Town Seafood was opened on Highland Road.

[signature]

F·I·S·H L·I·S·T

Mike Anderson's Seafood is synonymous with fresh seafood. How do we do it? Dedicated employees have been carefully trained to identify the freshest of the fresh seafood. If the seafood does not meet our standard of freshness, it is returned to the supplier. We receive seafood deliveries regularly. Fish is delivered daily.

The list below contains facts about some of the fish used in the restaurant. Each day a list of the fish available is posted so that customers may select which fish they would like us to use in the dish we prepare for them.

Many of the recipes in this cookbook ask for "fresh fish fillets" in the ingredients. Any of these fish can be used. Grill, broil, top and Enjoy!

MAHI MAHI

Description: This fish, with its silver markings, ranges in color from a yellowish to a metallic green, to a green gold or to even a dark blue. Mahi Mahi traditionally have an elongated body with flattened sides, and a dorsal fin that runs along the bottom of the fish ending at a forked tail.

Habitat: Mahi Mahi are known to roam in the blue offshore waters from snapper banks to the 100-fathom curve. These fish congregate around rigs, shrimp boats and floating seaweed. General fishing season begins in April and lasts until September.

Diet: Primarily a surface, feeding fish, Mahi Mahi are known to eat small fish.

Average Size: 4 to 10 pounds

REDFISH

Description: Redfish can be recognized by their blunt snout and square tail. They are reddish-bronze in color with at least one round or oval black spot on top of their tail.

Habitat: Adult fish, four years or older, spend most of their time in the Gulf. Younger Redfish can be found in bays, visiting oyster reefs and feeding near grass flats year round. They seek out shallow water areas that have a quick escape to deeper water.

Diet: Redfish enjoy dining on shrimp, crustaceans and other small fish.

Average Size: 3 to 8 pounds

BLACK DRUM

Description: Black Drum are gray or black in color with very large scales. Younger Drum are known to have vertical stripes. A high arched back and 10 to 14 pairs of chin barbells add to its distinguishing looks. Black Drum have cobblestone-like teeth capable of crushing oysters.

Habitat: Black Drum are found inshore and offshore around oyster beds. Known as a bottom dweller, bays and lagoons are another place this tasty fish can be spotted.

Diet: Black Drum eat oysters, mussels, crabs, shrimp and occasionally other fish.

Average Size: Up to 30 pounds

SPECKLED TROUT

Description: Speckled Trout are known for their streamlined bodies, grayish back and silvery sides, and the numerous black spots on the upper sides continuing along the dorsal fin to the tail fins. Speckled Trout have a yellow-orange color on the inside of their mouth along with 1 or 2 canine teeth in the upper jaw.

Habitat: Their domain includes bays, jetties, passes and the surf. Their location is often determined by the season. In winter months, Speckled Trout, can be found in deep holes. In the spring and fall they are found in shallower water. In the summer they seem to enjoy reefs and platforms.

Diet: Smaller species of Speckled Trout are known to feed on shrimp and small fish. As they grow, so do their taste buds. Two to three year old Speckled Trout prefer to dine mostly on other fish.

Average Size: 1 to 3 pounds

RED SNAPPER

Description: Red Snapper are easily identified by the most novice fisherman. They are a deep red color with a dark fringe around the dorsal and caudal fins.

Habitat: Red Snapper are regarded as one of the best tasting of all fish, and they support substantial commercial and recreational fishermen throughout the Gulf of Mexico. Although larger Red Snapper generally stay in deeper offshore waters, younger Snapper stray toward the shore, occasionally even being found around jetties. Snapper of all sizes tend to congregate around some type of underwater structure. Oil rigs, shipwrecks and reefs all provide fishermen with an excellent catch.

Diet: The bait of choice for most Snapper fishermen is squid. Red Snapper also enjoy feeding on crab, shrimp and other small fish. Because Snapper are bottom dwelling fish, heavy weights are used.

Average Size: 5 to 15 pounds

F·I·S·H L·I·S·T

FLOUNDER

Description: Flounder are known for their flat bodies. Capable of changing color patterns to match surroundings, Flounder frequently settle at the bottom of the ocean, always looking up in search of food. Gulf Flounder are usually smaller and more brownish in color than Southern Flounder. Gulf Flounder have three ocellated spots arranged in a triangular pattern on their topsides. Southern Flounder are more common than Gulf Flounder.

Habitat: (Southern and Gulf) Southern Flounder are the most abundant flatfish in the Texas waters. Both species are found in shallow water during warm months and then migrate through cuts and passes to the Gulf of Mexico to spawn during the fall and winter months. Flounder are ambush feeders and will wait patiently for dinner to swim by. Flounder sometimes bury themselves under sand or silt as they wait for food to enter the area. Prime fishing season is during the "Flounder Run" (spawning). Gigging is a popular method for catching Flounder. This is done by either wading with a bright light and "gigging" or spearing the fish with a multi pronged gig or using a flat bottom boat equipped with bright lights and spears.

Diet: Young Flounder feed on crustaceans; older Flounder eat mostly fish.

Average Size: 1 to 3 pounds (Southern)
less than 1 pound (Gulf)

SHEEPHEAD OR BAY SNAPPER

Description: Sheephead are basic silver with distinct black bands on each side. They also have prominent teeth that include incisors, molars and rounded grinders.

Habitat: Sheephead generally congregate around oyster bars, seawalls and in tidal creeks. In late winter and early spring during spawning, they move to artificial reefs, gathering debris and navigation markers.

Diet: Dinner normally consists of mollusks and crustaceans such as the fiddler crab and barnacles. Famed nibbler, the Sheephead prompted the saying, "Anglers must strike just before they bite."

Average Size: 1 to 2 pounds (inshore)
8 pounds (offshore)

18

POMPANO

Description: Starting with a gray-blue color on top, and shading to silver on the sides and to yellow on the bottom, Pompano have a deeply forked tail with smooth sides.

Habitat: This fish can usually be seen near sandy beaches, just inside the breakers. Primary fishing season is late in the spring through early fall. Pompano have small mouths and require using smaller bait and hooks.

Diet: Pompano, preferring to live near beaches, feed on mollusks, beach fleas, shrimp, small fish and crustaceans.

Average Size: 2 to 4 pounds

TUNA (BLUEFIN, YELLOWFIN, SKIPJACK)

Description:

Bluefin: This species of Tuna is dark blue at the top, shading to white on the sides and the bottom. They are known to have a heavy, blocky body that tapers to a slender forked tail.

Yellowfin: This species is more colorful than other Tuna. The breast and fins of the Tuna are yellowish in color. The second dorsal fin and anal fins are elongated.

Skipjack: Known for its greenish-blue shading along its silvery sides, and the dark stripes that run lengthwise along the bottom half of its chunky body, Skipjack blend well with the ocean colors. Its dorsal fins are close together, but separate.

Habitat:

Bluefin: This species of Tuna stays true to its name. It is most commonly found in blue water, far from shore. The best seasons for trying your luck with the Bluefin is spring and early summer.

Yellowfin: This fish makes its home in schools far off shore. However, they do come closer to shore than any other species of Tuna.

Skipjack: It is a rarity, but if seen, the Skipjack Tuna can be found during warm months, anywhere in the Gulf.

Diet:

Bluefin: Primarily feed on schooling fish.

Yellowfin/Skipjack: Flying fish, schooling fish as well as squid and crustaceans make up the dinners of this species of Tuna.

Average Size: **Bluefin:** 300 to 500 pounds
Yellowfin: up to 100 pounds
Skipjack: 3 to 6 pounds

MACKEREL (KING AND SPANISH)

Description: This long and slim bodied fish is also known as the Kingfisher. King Mackerel are gray and dull silver in color with white on the bottom and a scaled pectoral fin. Young King Mackerel possess yellow spots similar to Spanish Mackerel. The Spanish Mackerel are similar in color to the King, but have golden-yellow spots and a smooth pectoral fin.

Habitat:

King: Roaming in schools close to the shore or many miles out, seems to be the habit of the King Mackerel. Fishing season is generally May through October. The best place to test the waters for a chance at a King Mackerel is around tide lines, oil platforms, reefs and anchored shrimp boats.

Spanish: These fish roam in schools and congregate around the mouth of channels and passes. Fishing season begins in May and ends in September with August being the prime month.

Diet:

King: The King Mackerel dines primarily on other fish.

Spanish: Shrimp, squid and small fish are common choices of the Spanish Mackerel.

Average Size:

King: Regularly 8 to 12 pounds

Spanish: 15 to 18 inches, less than 2 pounds

SOME INFORMATION ABOUT SHRIMP

Shrimp, of all seafood, is by far the most popular. In the United States alone, more than half a billion pounds of shrimp are consumed each year. The shrimp in the Gulf of Mexico are among the best and most bountiful of the 2000 species found worldwide.

Shrimp are graded by number. Jumbo, 16 to 20 count. This means it takes 16 to 20 of these shrimp to equal one pound. I use this size shrimp in the Mike's Special, the Mike's Supreme and the Shrimp Cocktail. Large, 21 to 25 count. This, of course, means that it takes 21 to 25 of these shrimp to equal a pound. This size is used for my Fried Shrimp Platters. This continues with medium, 26 to 30 count, used for the Boiled Shrimp recipe, medium/small, 41 to 50 count, used to load up my shrimp poboys and loaves, and small/popcorn, 90 to 110 count, used for soups, salads and stuffing. Throughout this cookbook shrimp counts are used. Refer to this page at any time during cooking for help.

In purchasing shrimp and any seafood, freshness is my first and foremost requirement. My test for this is the use of my nose. This seems to work better than anything else. In dealing with fresh seafood a faint smell of ammonia is a red flag that spoilage is developing.

The Basics

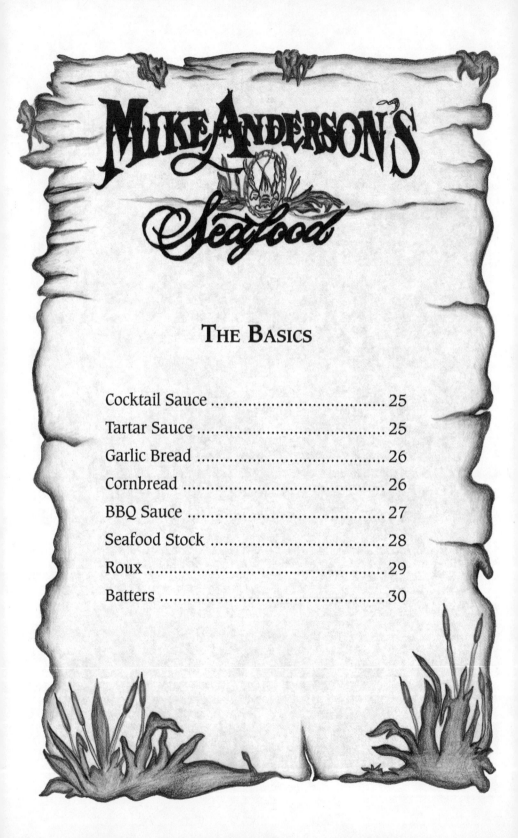

MIKE ANDERSON'S Seafood

THE BASICS

COCKTAIL SAUCE

1½ teaspoons prepared
    horseradish
1½ teaspoons
    Worcestershire sauce
¾ teaspoon hot sauce
¼ teaspoon salt
¼ teaspoon sugar

¼ teaspoon garlic
    powder
¾ teaspoon black pepper
¼ teaspoon fresh lemon
    juice
1⅓ cups ketchup

Mix all ingredients. Chill and serve.

Yield: 2 cups

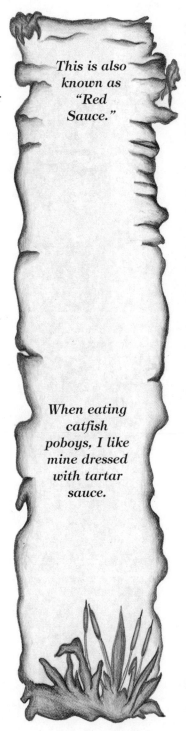

This is also known as "Red Sauce."

TARTAR SAUCE

½ cup finely chopped
    yellow onions
⅓ cup sweet relish

2 tablespoons dill relish
1 cup mayonnaise

Combine all ingredients. Chill and serve.

Yield: 2 cups

When eating catfish poboys, I like mine dressed with tartar sauce.

GARLIC BREAD

For convenience, make garlic butter ahead of time and store in your refrigerator.

4 sticks margarine or butter	¼ teaspoon cayenne pepper
1½ tablespoons fresh minced garlic	1 tablespoon parsley flakes
1½ teaspoons black pepper	French bread
1½ teaspoons white pepper	

In a small saucepan, melt margarine or butter. Mix all ingredients except bread together. Refrigerate to thicken. Stir well. Spread on one side of bread. Grill on stove or broil in oven over medium heat, being careful not to burn bread.

Yield: 2 cups of garlic butter, enough for 2 or more loaves of French bread

To serve this with our Red Beans and Rice or another dish, just add desired amount of sugar to the ingredients, and bake.

CORNBREAD

5 eggs	1½ sticks butter or margarine, melted
1 tablespoon baking powder	5 cups cornmeal
1 cup self-rising flour	5 cups low-fat milk

In a mixing bowl, combine all ingredients. Using a whisk, stir well. Pour batter into a nonstick 11x17-inch pan or line a baking dish with aluminum foil. Bake 30 minutes at 450°.

Serves 6 people

BBQ Sauce

2   cups ketchup
1   tablespoon hot sauce
2   tablespoons
    Worcestershire sauce
1½ tablespoons Heinz 57
    Steak Sauce
¼   cup brown sugar
½   teaspoon salt
1½ teaspoons crushed red
    pepper
1½ teaspoons fresh
    minced garlic
1½ teaspoons Mike
    Anderson's South
    Louisiana Seasoning
    or Season All
1   teaspoon cayenne
    pepper
5   tablespoons vegetable
    oil
½   cup finely chopped
    purple onions
5   tablespoons fresh
    lemon juice

Combine all ingredients. Stir well. Chill and serve.

Yield: 1 quart

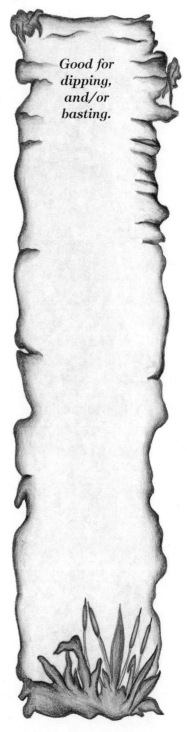

Good for dipping, and/or basting.

SEAFOOD STOCK

Because I use this in so many of my recipes, I always have some on hand. It is important when making this stock to use white fish, for example bones from black drum, redfish and snapper are good choices. Fish bones from tuna and salmon cause the stock to become oily.

2	pounds fish bones	3	stalks celery, chopped
1	whole onion, sliced	2	gallons water

In a large pot, combine all ingredients. Bring to a boil, then reduce heat to low, and simmer uncovered 2½ hours or more. Strain stock, discarding bones and vegetables.

Yield: 10 cups

ROUX

DARK ROUX

1½ cups cottonseed oil   2   cups self-rising flour

In a large saucepan, heat oil over high heat. Gradually add flour while continuing to stir. Cook over medium heat until dark brown.

Yield: 1¾ cups

LIGHT ROUX

4   sticks margarine or   2½ cups self-rising flour
       butter

In a large saucepan over medium heat, melt margarine or butter. Add flour while continuing to stir. Stir until mixture becomes a smooth paste. The roux will be yellow as it takes on the color of the margarine.

Yield: 4 cups

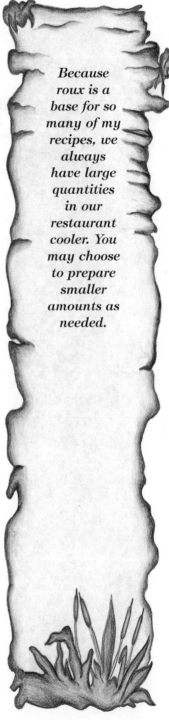

Because roux is a base for so many of my recipes, we always have large quantities in our restaurant cooler. You may choose to prepare smaller amounts as needed.

BATTERS

CRABFINGER BATTER

1½ cups self-rising flour
1 teaspoon salt

2 teaspoons cayenne
   pepper
1½ teaspoons granulated
   garlic

Combine all ingredients. Mix well. Store in cool, dry area.

Yield: 1½ cups

The Crabfinger Batter can be used when frying vegetables or just about anything else you like.

FISH BATTER

1¼ cups corn flour
½ cup cornmeal
1½ teaspoons salt
1 teaspoon cayenne
   pepper

2 teaspoons Mike
   Anderson's South
   Louisiana Seasoning
   or Season All

Combine all ingredients. Mix well. Store in cool, dry area.

Yield: 2 cups

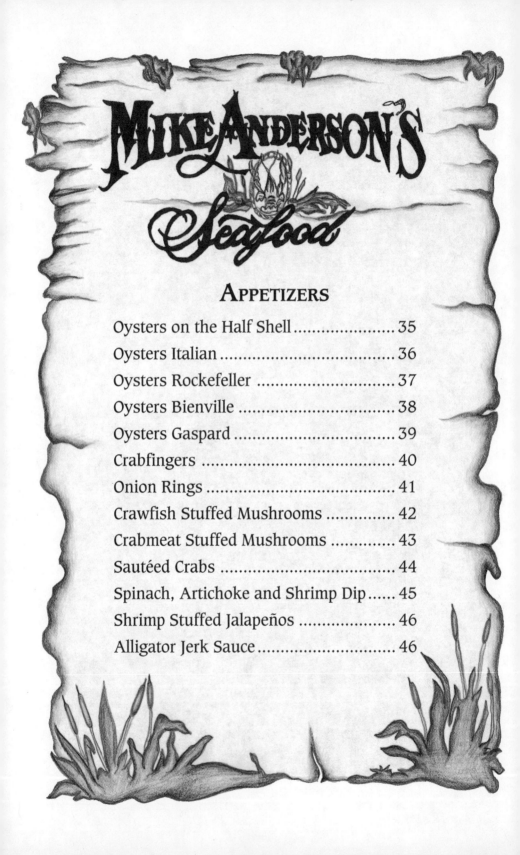

MIKE ANDERSON'S Seafood

APPETIZERS

THE "R" MYTH

Old-timers say that oysters should be eaten only in months with "R's" in them — September, October, etc. This is not true. Oysters can be consumed twelve months a year. The idea that oysters should not be eaten in months without the letter "r" in their spelling, (which happen to be the warm months in the south) was started many years ago before refrigerated trucks existed. Today, because of improved transportation and storage methods, we can enjoy oysters twelve months a year.

OYSTERS AND THEIR NUTRITIONAL VALUE

Oysters are not only delicious, but they are also one of the most nutritionally well-balanced foods, containing protein, carbohydrate and fat. The National Heart and Lung Institute suggests oysters as an ideal food for inclusion in low-cholesterol diets. Oysters are an excellent source of Vitamins A, B1, B2, B3, C and D. Four to five medium oysters supply the recommended daily allowance of iron, copper, iodine, magnesium, calcium, zinc, manganese and phosphorus.

HEALTH TIP

Because uncooked foods including oysters may carry bacteria, they should be avoided by pregnant women and persons with chronic liver disease, impaired immune systems or cancer.

How Do Pearls End Up Inside of the Oyster?

An oyster produces a pearl when foreign material becomes trapped inside the shell. The oyster responds to the irritation by producing nacre, a combination of calcium and protein. The nacre coats the foreign material, and over time, a pearl is produced.

How Oysters Breathe

Oysters breathe much like fish, using both gills and mantle. The mantle is lined with many small, thin-walled blood vessels, which extract oxygen from the water and expel carbon dioxide. A small, three-chambered heart, lying under the abductor muscle, pumps colorless blood, with its supply of oxygen, to all parts of the oyster body. At the same time, a pair of kidneys located on the underside of the muscle purify the blood of any waste products it has collected.

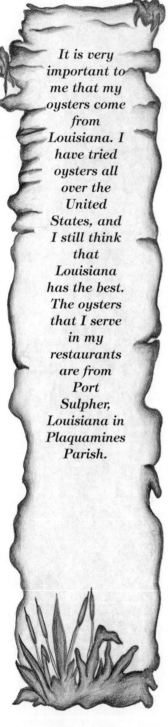

It is very important to me that my oysters come from Louisiana. I have tried oysters all over the United States, and I still think that Louisiana has the best. The oysters that I serve in my restaurants are from Port Sulpher, Louisiana in Plaquamines Parish.

OYSTERS ON THE HALF-SHELL

6-12 cold raw oysters 1 cocktail fork
1 cup Cocktail Sauce Saltine crackers (if desired)
  (See page 25)

Slide right onto a barstool and order. Tuesday night is "oyster night" at Mike Anderson's Seafood in Baton Rouge. Oysters are sold at a special price.

My favorite way to eat oysters is *"Rodeo" cold, straight out of the shell with a dash of hot sauce; but I highly recommend dipping them in my cocktail sauce.

*Rodeo— as cold as cold can get without freezing

OYSTERS ITALIAN

If you do not have oyster shells readily available, I suggest using a 3 to 4 ounce ramekin that can be purchased at any specialty food store. Friends tell me they have even used aluminum muffin tins. More fresh bread crumbs can be added to this recipe to make an oyster dressing.

1	dozen whole fresh oysters	1	teaspoon salt
1¾	cups chopped yellow onions	2	cups fresh oysters, coarsely chopped
1½	teaspoons fresh minced garlic	⅓	cup shredded Romano cheese
4	tablespoons butter or margarine	⅓	cup fresh Italian bread crumbs
½	teaspoon cayenne pepper	2	teaspoons parsley flakes
1	tablespoon granulated garlic		Grated Parmesan cheese

Boil or steam whole oysters for 2 to 3 minutes. Set aside. In a medium saucepan, sauté onions and minced garlic in butter or margarine. Cover and simmer for 15 minutes over low heat. Stir frequently. Add cayenne pepper, granulated garlic and salt. Stir well. Add chopped oysters. Cook over medium heat. When oysters begin to curl, add Romano cheese. Stir in bread crumbs and parsley. Spoon over whole oysters that have been placed in cleaned oyster shells. Sprinkle with Parmesan cheese and bake at 450° for 15 minutes or until Parmesan cheese is golden brown. If you are not serving right away, refrigerate and bake in oven at 450° for 40 minutes.

Serves 6 to 8 people

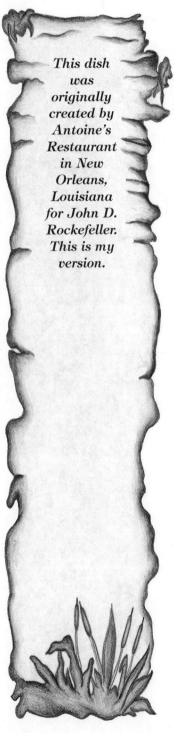

OYSTERS ROCKEFELLER

1	dozen whole fresh oysters	½	pound frozen chopped spinach, thawed and drained
1½	cups chopped yellow onions	1½	tablespoons finely chopped fresh anchovies
¼	cup finely chopped celery		
3	tablespoons butter or margarine	2½	tablespoons half-and-half
1¾	teaspoons sugar	¼	pound Velveeta cheese, cubed
½	teaspoon salt		
½	teaspoon cayenne pepper	5	tablespoons fresh bread crumbs, divided
¼	cup Pernod		

This dish was originally created by Antoine's Restaurant in New Orleans, Louisiana for John D. Rockefeller. This is my version.

Boil or steam whole oysters for 3 to 4 minutes. Set aside. In a medium saucepan, sauté onions and celery in butter or margarine. Cover and simmer for 15 to 20 minutes over low heat. Add sugar, salt, cayenne pepper and Pernod. Stir well. Add spinach and anchovies. Gradually add half-and-half. Stir. After spinach and milk have heated, add Velveeta cheese. Add 3 tablespoons bread crumbs. Stir well. Spoon over whole oysters that have been placed in cleaned oyster shells. Sprinkle with remaining 2 tablespoons bread crumbs and bake at 450° for 15 to 20 minutes. If you are not serving right away, refrigerate and bake for 45 minutes at 450°. Sprinkle bread crumbs just before baking.

Serves 6 to 8 people

OYSTERS BIENVILLE

Customers have shared with me that they have never come across a recipe for a Bienville that tastes like my version. I believe the addition of chopped oysters to the stuffing makes the difference.

½	cup finely chopped purple onions	1½	cups coarsely chopped fresh oysters
½	cup finely chopped green bell peppers	2	tablespoons self-rising flour
½	cup fresh chopped mushrooms	2	tablespoons cream sherry
1	teaspoon fresh minced garlic	2	tablespoons white wine
1	tablespoon seafood stock (See page 28)	⅓	cup heavy cream
		1	egg yolk
3	tablespoons butter or margarine	¼	cup shredded Romano cheese
¾	teaspoon salt	2	ounces white crabmeat (backfin)
¼	teaspoon cayenne pepper	⅓	cup fresh bread crumbs
½	teaspoon black pepper	¼	cup chopped green onions
½	pound fresh, peeled 90 to 110 count shrimp		

In a medium saucepan, sauté onions, bell peppers, mushrooms, garlic and seafood stock in butter or margarine. Cover and simmer for 10 to 15 minutes over low heat. Add salt, cayenne pepper and black pepper. Stir well. Using a food processor, chop shrimp. Add finely chopped shrimp and oysters to saucepan. Stir. In a separate bowl mix flour, cream sherry, white wine, heavy cream, egg yolk and Romano cheese. Set aside. When shrimp and oysters are halfway cooked, add crabmeat and cream mixture. Stir. Simmer over low heat until creamy. Add bread crumbs and green onions. Spoon into cleaned oyster shells. Bake at 450° for 15 to 20 minutes. If not serving right away, refrigerate and bake 40 minutes at 450°.

Serves 6 to 8 people

OYSTERS GASPARD

1	dozen whole fresh oysters	1	tablespoon Mike Anderson's South Louisiana Seasoning or Season All
12	slices uncooked bacon		
2¼	cups BBQ Sauce (See page 27)	1½	cups shredded mozzarella cheese

Boil or steam whole oysters for 2 to 3 minutes. Individually wrap each oyster with 1 slice of bacon. Bake in cleaned oyster shells at 450° for 3 minutes. Drain. Repeat this step until bacon is crispy. Top each oyster with 3 tablespoons of BBQ sauce. Sprinkle Mike Anderson's South Louisiana Seasoning or Season All over each oyster. Bake 10 to 15 minutes. Top each oyster with 2 tablespoons of mozzarella cheese. Bake at 450° until cheese is melted.

Serves 6 to 8 people

If you want to spice up this recipe a bit, add sliced jalapeño peppers on top of the BBQ sauce. Serve this dish hot while the mozzarella cheese is nice and gooey. That's how we do it!

CRABFINGERS

FRIED CRABFINGERS

1½ cups self-rising flour	1½ teaspoons granulated garlic
1 teaspoon salt	½ pound fresh crabfingers
2 teaspoons cayenne pepper	Cottonseed oil

Mix flour, salt, cayenne pepper and garlic together. Dip fresh crabfingers in water then in flour mixture. Repeat this step. Fry 4 to 6 minutes at 350° in cottonseed oil.

Serves 2 to 4 people

Marinated Crabfingers work well for party trays.

MARINATED CRABFINGERS

1 tablespoon vegetable oil	⅓ cup shredded Romano cheese
1 tablespoon water	1½ teaspoons prepared horseradish
2 tablespoons white vinegar	1½ teaspoons Worcestershire sauce
1¼ tablespoons sugar	½ teaspoon hot sauce
1 tablespoon fresh minced garlic	½ teaspoon salt
1 tablespoon fresh chopped green onion	¼ teaspoon fresh lemon juice
½ teaspoon black pepper	1⅓ cups ketchup
1¾ tablespoons granulated garlic	½ pound fresh crabfingers
1½ tablespoons grated Parmesan cheese	

Mix all ingredients and refrigerate 1 hour to marinate. On a bed of lettuce, arrange marinated crabfingers in a circle. Cover crabfingers with marinade. Serve chilled.

Yield: 2 cups marinade, ½ pound crabfingers

SAUTÉED CRABFINGERS

4	tablespoons margarine or butter	¼	teaspoon parsley flakes
½	tablespoon fresh lemon juice	¼	pound fresh crabfingers
¾	teaspoon Mike Anderson's South Louisiana Seasoning or Season All		

Mix all ingredients except crabfingers in a small saucepan. Cook until hot. Add crabfingers. Sauté until tender. Before serving add a pinch of parsley.

I also use the Mike's Supreme Sauce to sauté crabfingers. See page 76.

ONION RINGS

1	jumbo yellow onion	Self-rising flour
Water		Cottonseed oil

Peel and core onion. Cut onion into ½- to ¾-inch slices. Separate into rings. Soak rings in cold water until ready to use. Dip each ring in water then flour. Repeat this step. Heat cottonseed oil to 350°. Fry onion rings 3 to 4 minutes on both sides.

The Onion Rings are the only item I allow my waitstaff to bring out without a tray because of the delicate way they are stacked.

CRAWFISH STUFFED MUSHROOMS

In my restaurant these are served on the Crawfish 7-way dinner.

3 cups chopped yellow onions
5 cups chopped fresh mushrooms
1⅓ tablespoons fresh minced garlic
2½ sticks margarine or butter, divided
2 teaspoons salt
¼ teaspoon cayenne pepper
1 teaspoon white pepper
1¼ teaspoons black pepper
⅓ cup white wine
2 pounds crawfish tails
¾ cup fresh bread crumbs
24 fresh jumbo mushroom caps
Grated Parmesan cheese

In a small saucepan, sauté onions, mushrooms and garlic in 1½ sticks margarine or butter. Cover and simmer 15 to 20 minutes over low heat. Add all seasonings and white wine. Using a food processor, finely chop crawfish tails and add to mixture. Cook until crawfish are hot. Add bread crumbs. Stir well. Fill each mushroom cap with stuffing. Melt remaining 1 stick margarine or butter, and pour into a casserole dish. Place mushrooms in margarine or butter. Sprinkle with Parmesan cheese. Broil on high 2 to 4 minutes. If refrigerated, broil on high 8 minutes.

Serves 6 to 8 people

CRABMEAT STUFFED MUSHROOMS

¾ cup chopped yellow onions

¾ cup chopped fresh mushrooms

1½ sticks margarine or butter, divided

¼ teaspoon salt

⅛ teaspoon cayenne pepper

1½ teaspoons granulated garlic

¼ pound crabmeat (claw)

1½ tablespoons chopped green onions

1½ teaspoons parsley flakes

1 tablespoon fresh Italian bread crumbs

24 fresh jumbo mushroom caps

Grated Parmesan cheese

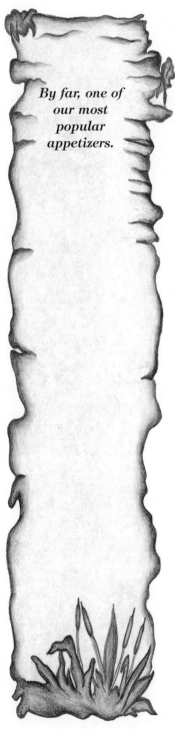

By far, one of our most popular appetizers.

In a medium saucepan, sauté onions and mushrooms in ½ stick margarine or butter. Cover and simmer 15 to 20 minutes over low heat. Stir frequently. Add salt, cayenne pepper and garlic. Stir. Add crabmeat. Cover and simmer 12 minutes. Add green onions, parsley and bread crumbs. Mix well. Fill each mushroom cap with stuffing. Melt remaining 1 stick margarine or butter, and pour into a baking dish. Place mushrooms in margarine or butter. Broil on high 4 minutes. If refrigerated, broil on high 8 minutes. Sprinkle with Parmesan cheese before serving.

Serves 6 to 8 people

SAUTÉED CRABS

6	tablespoons fresh minced garlic	1	teaspoon salt
¼	cup vegetable oil or olive oil	1	teaspoon sugar
3	fresh boiled crabs	½	tablespoon chopped green onions or parsley flakes
1	teaspoon black pepper		

In a medium saucepan, sauté garlic in vegetable oil until golden brown. Discard the back of the crabs and clean thoroughly. Chop boiled crabs into quarters (do not include small legs). Add crabs, pepper, salt and sugar to saucepan. Sauté until crabs are heated and seasoning is evenly dispersed. Top with your preference of green onions or parsley before serving.

Serves 2 to 4 people

BBQ CRABS

1	cup BBQ Sauce (See page 27)	3	fresh boiled crabs

Discard the back of the crabs and clean thoroughly. Chop boiled crabs into quarters (do not include small legs). Cover crabs in BBQ sauce. Broil on high until BBQ sauce begins to brown at edges.

Serves 2 to 4 people

SPINACH, ARTICHOKE AND SHRIMP DIP

3½ teaspoons fresh minced garlic
¼ cup olive oil
3½ cups chopped yellow onions
1 cup chopped artichoke hearts
6 jalapeño slices, chopped
1⅓ tablespoons jalapeño juice
2½ teaspoons black pepper

2¾ tablespoons light roux or self-rising flour (See page 29)
¾ pound frozen chopped spinach, thawed and drained
1 cup half-and-half
1 pound Velveeta cheese, cubed
½ pound boiled, peeled 90 to 110 count shrimp, finely chopped

Melba toast is easy to make, just thinly slice a loaf of French bread and toast in the oven. This dish may also be served as a casserole.

Sauté garlic in oil until golden brown. Add onions. Cover and simmer 15 to 20 minutes over low heat. Add artichoke hearts, jalapeños, jalapeño juice and black pepper. After the artichoke hearts start to break apart, add light roux. Stir well. Add spinach. Gradually stir in half-and-half. Slowly heat. Add Velveeta cheese and stir until melted. Add chopped shrimp and stir. Serve with chips or melba toast.

Serves 6 to 8

SHRIMP STUFFED JALAPEÑOS

Even though jalapeños are used, this dish is not overly spicy because the seeds are removed.

1 dozen fresh jalapeños
1½ cups shredded
    mozzarella cheese

12 fresh, peeled 16 to 20
    count shrimp,
    butterflied
Cottonseed oil

Steam or boil the jalapeños until tender. Cut in half and clean out seeds and center. Stuff 2 tablespoons cheese into each of 12 jalapeño halves. Open butterflied shrimp and place on top of cheese. Place remaining 12 jalapeño halves on top of the 12 stuffed halves. Dip in water then flour. Repeat this step. Fry 6 to 8 minutes in 350° cottonseed oil. Serve with ranch or blue cheese dressing.

Serves 6 to 8 people

ALLIGATOR JERK SAUCE

Jerk Sauce can also be used as a basting sauce for poultry, pork or beef.

½ cup Caribbean Jerk
    seasoning
1 cup chopped yellow
    onions
2 tablespoons fresh
    finely minced garlic
3 tablespoons soy sauce

3 tablespoons soybean
    oil
1 tablespoon balsamic
    vinegar
1¼ cups BBQ Sauce
    (See page 27)
Finger-size alligator strips
    (tail meat)

Add all ingredients except alligator strips to a blender. Blend well. Grill alligator strips. Heat sauce. Coat grilled alligator strips with sauce and serve.

Yield: about 2 cups sauce

Soups

SEAFOOD GUMBO

4	tablespoons vegetable oil	1	(10 ounce) can diced Rotel tomatoes, drained
1¼	tablespoons fresh minced garlic	11	cups water
3	cups chopped yellow onions	½	pound crabmeat (claw)
½	cup chopped green bell peppers	¾	cup sliced okra (boiled in vinegar and water), drained
¾	cup chopped celery	½	pound white crabmeat (backfin)
1½	tablespoons salt	¼	cup chopped green onions
½	teaspoon cayenne pepper	½	pound fresh, peeled 90 to 110 count shrimp
2	bay leaves		
½	cup dark roux (See page 29)		
2½	tablespoons seafood stock (See page 28)		

In a small saucepan, sauté garlic in vegetable oil until golden brown. In large pot combine yellow onions, bell peppers, celery, and sautéed garlic. Cover and simmer 10 to 15 minutes over low heat. Add salt, cayenne pepper, bay leaves, dark roux and seafood stock. Stir. Add Rotel tomatoes and water. Stir. Add claw crabmeat. Cook gumbo over low heat for 1 hour or more. Add okra, white crabmeat, green onions and shrimp. Cover and cook until shrimp are done. Serve over rice.

Serves 6 to 8 people

More roux may be added to adjust the color and consistency of gumbo. Gumbo is even better the next day after storing in the refrigerator. Reheat slowly. My mother-in-law, Vina Gaspard, made the original gumbo. I have added to it over the years, but the basics have remained the same.

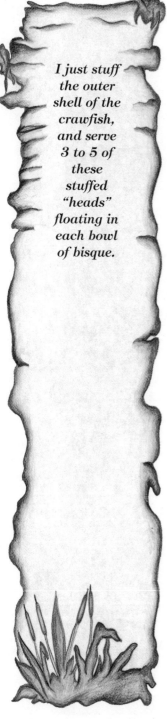

CRAWFISH BISQUE

HEAD STUFFING

I just stuff the outer shell of the crawfish, and serve 3 to 5 of these stuffed "heads" floating in each bowl of bisque.

3 cups chopped yellow onions	1¼ teaspoons salt
1¼ cups chopped green bell peppers	1⅛ teaspoons cayenne pepper
¾ cups chopped celery	1⅛ teaspoons crushed red pepper
2¼ teaspoons fresh minced garlic	1 pound crawfish tails
¼ cup seafood stock (See page 28)	1½ cups chopped green onions
2 sticks margarine or butter	2 cups crumbled cornbread (See page 26)

Using a small saucepan, sauté yellow onions, bell peppers, celery, garlic and seafood stock in margarine or butter. Cover and simmer 20 to 30 minutes over low heat. Stir frequently. Add salt, cayenne pepper and crushed red pepper. Stir well. Using a food processor, finely chop crawfish tails and add to saucepan. Cook until hot. Add green onions and cornbread. Stir. Refrigerate until ready for stuffing.

Yield: 7 cups

CRAWFISH BISQUE

6	cups chopped yellow onions	2½	cups head stuffing (See page 50)
¾	cup chopped green bell peppers	¼	cup dark roux (See page 29)
½	cup chopped celery	5	cups water
¼	cup seafood stock (See page 28)	2¾	teaspoons hot sauce
1	tablespoon fresh minced garlic	3¼	tablespoons chopped green onions
4	tablespoons margarine or butter	1	tablespoon parsley flakes
2½	teaspoons salt	1	pound crawfish tails
½	teaspoon cayenne pepper	36	crawfish heads stuffed with 4½ cups head stuffing (See page 50)

In a large pot, sauté yellow onions, bell peppers, celery, seafood stock and garlic in margarine or butter. Cover and simmer 30 minutes over low heat. Stir frequently. Add salt, cayenne pepper, head stuffing and dark roux. Stir. Add water and hot sauce. Boil 3 to 4 minutes then lower heat. Add green onions, parsley and crawfish tails. Cook over low heat until crawfish are hot. Add stuffed heads. Serve over rice.

Serves 6 to 8 people

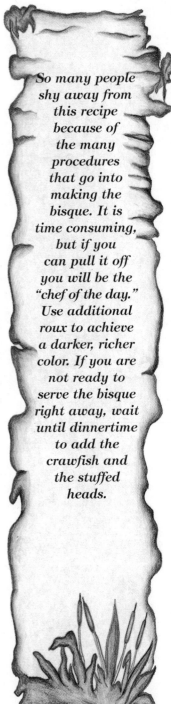

So many people shy away from this recipe because of the many procedures that go into making the bisque. It is time consuming, but if you can pull it off you will be the "chef of the day." Use additional roux to achieve a darker, richer color. If you are not ready to serve the bisque right away, wait until dinnertime to add the crawfish and the stuffed heads.

CRAWFISH ÉTOUFFÉE

The color of the étouffée is directly affected by the fat content of the crawfish tails. At the restaurant, I drain off part of the fat, reserving just enough for the required color and flavor. At the Baton Rouge location, we use this étouffée as a topping on Friday's lunch special, The Lefete. (See page 109).

1   stick margarine or butter
12   cups chopped yellow onions
1   cup chopped green bell peppers
¾   cup chopped celery
2   teaspoons fresh minced garlic
1½   tablespoons seafood stock (See page 28)
1¼   tablespoons salt
1½   teaspoons black pepper

1¼   cups light roux (See page 29)
1   (10-ounce) can diced Rotel tomatoes, drained
1   teaspoon granulated garlic
3¾   cups water
1   pound crawfish tails
2   tablespoons parsley flakes

In a medium pot, combine margarine or butter, onions, bell peppers, celery and minced garlic. Add seafood stock. Cover and simmer 45 minutes over low heat. Stir frequently. Add salt, pepper, roux, Rotel tomatoes, garlic and water. Bring to a boil. Stir constantly. Add crawfish tails. Cook 15 minutes. Add parsley. Stir well. Serve over rice.

Serves 6 to 8 people

SHRIMP STEW

5½	cups finely chopped yellow onions	¼	teaspoon cayenne pepper
2	cups finely chopped green bell peppers	1	cup light roux (See page 29)
1	cup finely chopped celery	½	pound white crabmeat (backfin)
4	tablespoons butter or margarine	8	cups water
3¼	teaspoons salt	½	pound fresh, peeled 90 to 110 count shrimp

In a medium pot, sauté onions, bell peppers and celery in butter or margarine. Cover and simmer 30 minutes over low heat. Stir frequently. Add salt, cayenne pepper and light roux. Stir. Add crabmeat. Gradually stir in water. Cook for 1 hour over low heat. Add shrimp. Cook until shrimp are done. Serve over rice.

Serves 6 to 8 people

When cooking in large quantities at the restaurant, the veggies keep their natural color. At home you may find with this condensed recipe, the veggies turn a little darker. Don't worry, this does not effect the taste.

CRABMEAT ÉTOUFFÉE

The
Crabmeat
Étouffée is
also used to
top the
Normans
(See page
107 and
108). These
are two of
my oldest
dishes and
remain
bestsellers.

6	cups chopped yellow onions
¾	cup chopped green bell peppers
½	cup chopped celery
2½	teaspoons fresh minced garlic
4	tablespoons butter
4	tablespoons margarine
2½	teaspoons salt
½	teaspoon cayenne pepper
1¾	cups light roux (See page 29)
4	cups water, divided
1½	pounds white crabmeat (lump or backfin), divided

In a medium pot, sauté onions, bell peppers, celery and garlic in butter and margarine. Cover and simmer 30 minutes over low heat. Stir frequently. Add salt, cayenne pepper and light roux. Stir. Simmer 5 to 7 minutes over medium heat. Add ½ cup water. Bring to a boil. Add remaining water. Add 1 pound of crabmeat. Bring to a boil. Add remaining crabmeat and heat before serving. Serve over rice.

Serves 6 to 8 people

RED BEANS AND RICE

4	cups red beans, dry	1	tablespoon salt
6	cups chopped yellow onions	1	teaspoon cayenne pepper
1¼	cups chopped green bell peppers	2	teaspoons black pepper
½	cup chopped celery	1	pound smoked sausage, sliced
1½	teaspoons fresh minced garlic	¾	pound ham, cubed
8	cups water		

Soak red beans in water overnight. Rinse and drain beans and pour into a medium pot. Add onions, bell peppers, celery, garlic and water. Cover and simmer 45 minutes to 1 hour over medium heat. Add salt, cayenne pepper and black pepper. Stir well. Add sausage and ham. Cook over low heat until beans are done. Serve over rice.

Serves 6 to 8 people

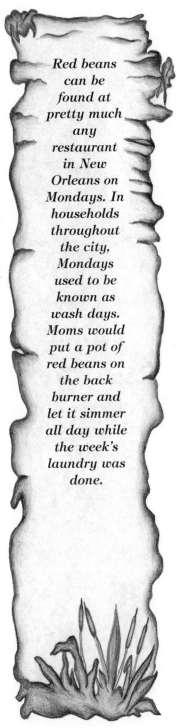

Red beans can be found at pretty much any restaurant in New Orleans on Mondays. In households throughout the city, Mondays used to be known as wash days. Moms would put a pot of red beans on the back burner and let it simmer all day while the week's laundry was done.

SHRIMP CREOLE

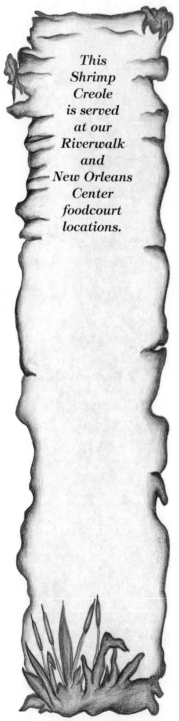

This Shrimp Creole is served at our Riverwalk and New Orleans Center foodcourt locations.

1½	sticks margarine or butter	1	(6-ounce) can tomato paste
12	cups chopped yellow onions	1	(10-ounce) can diced Rotel tomatoes, drained
¾	cup chopped green bell peppers	1¾	tablespoons red wine
1	cup chopped celery	½	teaspoon cayenne pepper
1¼	teaspoons fresh minced garlic	1	tablespoon sugar
3	cups water	4¾	teaspoons salt
1¼	tablespoons dark roux (See page 29)	½	pound fresh, peeled 90 to 110 count shrimp
1	(8-ounce) can tomato sauce		

In a large pot, combine margarine or butter, onions, bell peppers, celery, garlic and water. Cover and simmer 45 minutes over low heat. Add dark roux, tomato sauce, tomato paste, Rotel tomatoes and red wine. Bring to a boil. Add cayenne pepper, sugar and salt. Add shrimp. Cook over low heat until shrimp are done. Serve over rice.

Serves 6 to 8 people

REDFISH COURTBOUILLION

9	cups chopped yellow onions	1	tablespoon salt	
5	cups chopped green bell peppers	5	(8-ounce) cans tomato sauce	
1½	tablespoons fresh minced garlic	3	(6-ounce) cans tomato paste	
1½	sticks margarine or butter	2	(10-ounce) cans diced Rotel tomatoes, drained	
3	tablespoons chicken base	2½	tablespoons dark roux (See page 29)	
1¾	teaspoons granulated garlic	3	pounds fresh fish fillets, diced	

In a large pot, sauté onions, bell peppers and minced garlic in margarine or butter. Cover and simmer 30 to 45 minutes over low heat. Add chicken base, granulated garlic and salt. Stir well. Add tomato sauce, tomato paste, Rotel tomatoes and dark roux. Bring to a boil. Add diced fish fillets. Cook over low heat until fish are done. Serve over rice.

Serves 6 to 8 people

By definition "courtbouillon" refers to a poaching liquid flavored with onions and various spices. In south Louisiana the vegetables and spices play an important part in the recipe, but not as much as the rich roux base of the tomato sauce. Different kinds of fish may be used depending on the season. For variety, batter and fry fish before adding to sauce.

ALLIGATOR SAUCE PIQUANT

FRIED ALLIGATOR

2½ pounds alligator meat, cubed	Flour
	Cottonseed oil

Dip alligator meat in water then flour. Repeat this step. Heat cottonseed oil to 350°. Fry alligator meat 3 to 4 minutes. Drain.

SAUCE

6	cups chopped yellow onions	2½	teaspoons sugar
⅓	cup chopped green bell peppers	3	(8-ounce) cans tomato sauce
1	cup chopped celery	3	(10-ounce) cans diced Rotel tomatoes, drained
2	teaspoons fresh minced garlic	1	cup draft light beer
1	stick margarine or butter	½	cup red wine
2	teaspoons salt	2½	teaspoons dark roux (See page 29)
¼	teaspoon cayenne pepper	2½	pounds fried alligator

In a large pot, sauté onions, bell peppers, celery and garlic in margarine or butter. Cover and simmer 15 to 20 minutes over low heat. Add salt, cayenne pepper and sugar. Stir well. Add remaining ingredients. Bring to a boil. Add fried alligator. Simmer over low heat until ready to serve. Serve over rice.

Serves 6 to 8 people

I always make it a point to serve this dish the weekend we play the Florida Gators, whether the game is at home or away.

OYSTER, SPINACH AND ARTICHOKE BISQUE

2	sticks butter or margarine	½	teaspoon Mike Anderson's South Louisiana Seasoning or Season All
2	bay leaves		
2½	cups chopped yellow onions		
2½	teaspoons fresh minced garlic	2½	tablespoons chicken base
1¼	cups canned artichoke hearts, quartered	3¼	tablespoons white wine
1¼	cups chopped fresh mushrooms	1	cup condensed cream of mushroom soup
1¾	teaspoons black pepper	2¼	cups water
¼	teaspoon thyme	½	cup self-rising flour
		8	cups fresh oysters, coarsely chopped
		½	pound chopped frozen spinach, thawed and drained

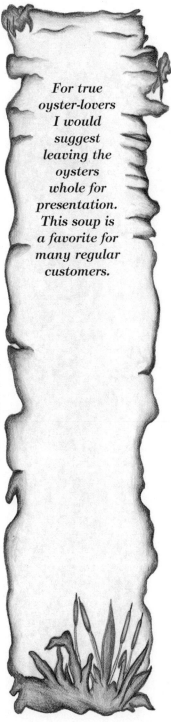

For true oyster-lovers I would suggest leaving the oysters whole for presentation. This soup is a favorite for many regular customers.

In a medium pot, combine butter or margarine, bay leaves, onions and garlic. Sauté until garlic is golden brown. Add artichoke hearts, mushrooms, pepper, thyme, Mike Anderson's South Louisiana Seasoning or Season All and chicken base. Stir. In a separate bowl, mix wine, cream of mushroom soup, water and flour. Add soup mixture to pot. Stir well. Add chopped oysters. Cook over low heat until oysters are firm. Add spinach. Cook until creamy.

Serves 6 to 8 people

CRAB AND CORN BISQUE

Once, at home, I added bite-sized pieces of a smoked ham that I had cooked the day before. This really enhanced the flavor of the bisque.

8	cups chopped yellow onions	½	cup self-rising flour
1	stick margarine or butter	3½	cups half-and-half
2¾	teaspoons salt	5	cups low-fat milk
½	teaspoon cayenne pepper	1	(15¼-ounce) can whole kernel corn, drained
¼	teaspoon white pepper	1	pound white crabmeat (lump or backfin)
2¼	teaspoons granulated garlic		

In a medium pot, sauté onions in margarine or butter. Cover and simmer 15 to 20 minutes over low heat. Stir frequently. Add salt, cayenne pepper, white pepper, garlic and flour. Stir well. Gradually add half-and-half and milk. Stir. Bring to a boil. Add corn and crabmeat. Lower heat and cook until creamy.

Serves 6 to 8 people

TURTLE SOUP

3	cups chopped yellow onions	3	bay leaves
2	carrots, shredded	2¼	teaspoons ground thyme
¾	cup chopped celery	1½	tablespoons dried basil
¾	cup chopped green bell peppers	1¼	tablespoons salt
1¼	tablespoons fresh minced garlic	1½	teaspoons black pepper
1	(10-ounce) can diced Rotel tomatoes	1½	tablespoons Worcestershire sauce
1¾	cups white wine	5	tablespoons Tiger Sauce*
2½	tablespoons chicken base	6	cups water
1½	pounds turtle meat, cubed	4	boiled eggs, sliced
		½	cup parsley flakes

In a large pot combine onions, carrots, celery, bell peppers and garlic. Cover and simmer 10 to 15 minutes, using low heat to avoid burning. Stir frequently. Add Rotel tomatoes, white wine, chicken base and turtle meat. Add bay leaves, thyme, basil, salt, black pepper, Worcestershire sauce and Tiger Sauce. Stir. Add water. Cook over medium heat until turtle meat is tender. Pour mixture through strainer, saving stock. Remove bay leaves. Using a food processor, chop strained mixture. Combine with stock. Simmer over low heat until ready to serve. Add egg slices and parsley before serving.

Serves 6 to 8 people

*If you have difficulty finding Tiger Sauce, try www.tigersauce.com

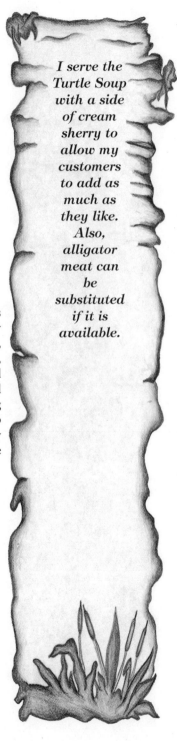

I serve the Turtle Soup with a side of cream sherry to allow my customers to add as much as they like. Also, alligator meat can be substituted if it is available.

SEAFOOD CHOWDER

BOILED POTATOES

2 teaspoons liquid crab boil
4 cups water

3 medium potatoes, peeled

In a medium pot, combine crab boil and water. Bring to a boil. Add potatoes. Cook over high heat until potatoes are tender. Drain and set aside.

CHOWDER

3-4 slices bacon
4 cups chopped yellow onions
1½ cups chopped green bell peppers
1 tablespoon salt
½ teaspoon black pepper
1 teaspoon cayenne pepper

1 teaspoon ground thyme
1 pound crawfish tails
1½ pounds fresh, peeled 90 to 110 count shrimp
4 cups low-fat milk

Fry bacon until well done. Set aside. Reserve bacon fat. In a medium pot, sauté onions and bell peppers in reserved fat. Cover and simmer 15 to 20 minutes over low heat. Quarter previously boiled potatoes. Add potatoes, salt, black pepper, cayenne pepper and thyme. Stir. Add crawfish, shrimp and bacon. Stir. Cook over medium heat until shrimp are done. Add milk. Simmer until creamy.

Serves 6 to 8 people

During refrigeration, chowder may thicken. When this occurs, I add a small amount of milk when reheating and stir until desired consistency. Thyme is the ingredient that gives this chowder its unique taste.

Vegetable Soup with Shrimp and Crabmeat

Boiled Potatoes

1	teaspoon liquid crab boil	2	medium potatoes, peeled
3	cups water		

In a medium pot, combine crab boil and water. Bring to a boil. Add potatoes. Cook over high heat until potatoes are tender. Drain and set aside.

Soup

1	stick margarine or butter	1	tablespoon salt
3½	cups chopped yellow onions	1¼	teaspoons cayenne pepper
1	cup chopped green bell peppers	6	cups water
¼	head green cabbage, thinly sliced	½	(15¼-ounce) can whole kernel corn, drained
½	cup seafood stock (See page 28)	½	pound crabmeat (claw)
1	(10-ounce) can diced Rotel tomatoes, drained	1¼	pounds fresh, peeled 90 to 110 count shrimp
1¼	teaspoons granulated garlic	1	carrot, shredded

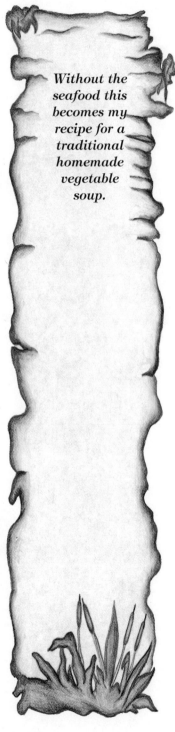

Without the seafood this becomes my recipe for a traditional homemade vegetable soup.

In a large pot, combine margarine or butter, onions, bell peppers, cabbage and seafood stock. Cover and simmer 30 minutes over low heat. Stir frequently. Quarter previously boiled potatoes. Add potatoes, Rotel tomatoes, granulated garlic, salt, cayenne pepper and water. Simmer over low heat 30 to 45 minutes. Add corn, crabmeat, shrimp and carrots. Stir. Cook over medium heat until shrimp are done.

Serves 6 to 8 people

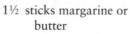

BROCCOLI AND CRABMEAT SOUP

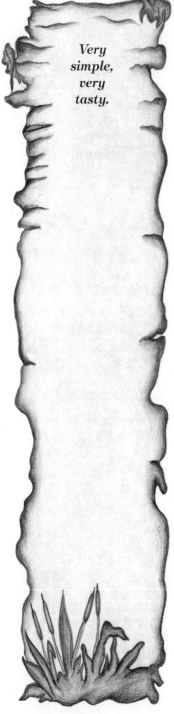

Very simple, very tasty.

1½ sticks margarine or butter
6   cups chopped yellow onions
1¾ tablespoons salt
2¾ teaspoons white pepper

1   cup self-rising flour
12 cups low-fat milk
2   fresh broccoli heads, chopped
1   pound white crabmeat (lump)

In a large pot, combine margarine or butter and onions. Cover and simmer 15 to 20 minutes over low heat. Stir frequently. Add salt, white pepper and flour. Stir. Gradually add milk. Stir. Add chopped broccoli. Cook until broccoli is tender. Add crabmeat. Gently stir. Simmer 2 to 3 more minutes and serve.

Serves 6 to 8 people.

KING CRAB SOUP

9	cups chopped yellow onions	1¾	teaspoons fresh lemon juice
1¾	cups chopped green bell peppers	1¼	tablespoons light roux (See page 29)
¾	cup chopped celery	⅓	cup self-rising flour
1½	sticks margarine or butter	3	cups half-and-half
1¼	tablespoons salt	9	cups low-fat milk
1¾	teaspoons white pepper	1¼	pounds white crabmeat (lump or
1¾	teaspoons Worcestershire sauce	3	backfin) boiled crabs, chopped

In a large pot, sauté onions, bell peppers and celery in margarine or butter. Cover and simmer 30 minutes over low heat. Stir frequently. Add salt, white pepper, Worcestershire sauce and lemon juice. Stir. Add light roux and flour. Gradually stir half-and-half and milk into saucepan. Simmer over low heat until creamy. Add crabmeat and boiled crabs. Cook until hot.

Serves 6 to 8 people

The boiled crabs add both color and flavor to this soup. We first prepared this soup around the time of Mardi Gras when kings and queens ride the streets of New Orleans on Mardi Gras floats, hence the name King Crab Soup.

CREOLE GUMBO

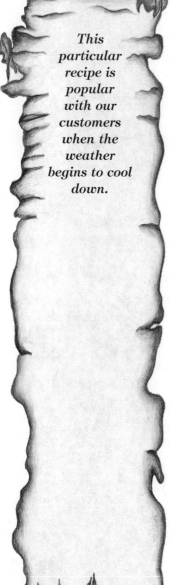

This particular recipe is popular with our customers when the weather begins to cool down.

1¼ tablespoons fresh minced garlic
¼ cup vegetable oil
3 cups chopped yellow onions
½ cup chopped green bell peppers
¾ cup chopped celery
1½ tablespoons salt
½ teaspoon cayenne pepper
2 bay leaves
½ cup dark roux (See page 29)
2½ tablespoons seafood stock (See page 28)
1 (10-ounce) can diced Rotel tomatoes, drained

11 cups water
½ pound crabmeat (claw)
¾ cup sliced okra (boiled in vinegar and water), drained
½ pound white crabmeat (backfin)
¼ cup chopped green onions
½ pound fresh, peeled 90 to 110 count shrimp
½ pound boneless, skinless chicken, cut into strips
¾ pound smoked sausage, sliced

In a small saucepan, sauté garlic in vegetable oil until golden brown. In a large pot combine yellow onions, bell peppers, celery and sautéed garlic. Cover and simmer 10 to 15 minutes over low heat. Add salt, cayenne pepper, bay leaves, dark roux and seafood stock. Stir. Add Rotel tomatoes and water. Stir. Add claw crabmeat. Cook gumbo over low heat for 1 hour or more. Add okra, white crabmeat, green onions, shrimp, chicken and smoked sausage. Cover and cook until shrimp are done. Serve over rice.

Serves 6 to 8 people

FRIED SEAFOOD

J. JEFFREY '99

Mike Anderson's Seafood

Fried Seafood

MIKE ANDERSON ON FRIED SEAFOOD

There is an art to frying seafood. It is more than just battering something and dropping it into hot oil. "Keep the shrimp at a golden brown." "Rough-up those rings." "Make sure the oysters are not too hard." "Don't let the oil burn." "Where is your thermometer?" These are only a few statements that are heard throughout the kitchen on any given night. I've been told that one of the main reasons people come to my restaurants is for the quality of our fried seafood. Well, it doesn't come easily. It involves constant training and supervision. It all boils down to two things, oil and practice. OIL. Is it the right temperature? Is it filtered properly? Is it discarded when it gets old? We use cottonseed oil because we do a lot of frying, and because it doesn't burn easily. For your use, any peanut or vegetable oil will do. PRACTICE. One must practice, practice, practice. I have a certain look I try to achieve with my fried items. Basically, I like most of my fried food to look roughed-up. I hope that is what you receive and enjoy when the finished product hits your table. Here are the techniques we use in my restaurants.

FRIED SEAFOOD

FRIED SHRIMP

Fresh, peeled shrimp, butterflied
Water

Self-rising flour
Cottonseed oil

Dip shrimp in water, then flour. When doing this, rub shrimp with your fingertips (this achieves the roughed-up look), dip back in water, then flour. Heat oil to 350°. Place shrimp in oil. Fry 4 to 6 minutes.

FRIED OYSTERS

Fresh oysters
Fish Batter (See page 30)

Cottonseed oil

Pull the oysters straight out of the chilled gallon. Place oysters in Fish Batter. Shake off excess batter. Heat oil to 350°. Fry oysters 4 to 5 minutes. I like a little firmness when eating fried oysters. But, be careful. They can overcook in a split second.

FRIED CATFISH FILLETS

Fresh catfish fillets
Fish Batter (See page 30)

Cottonseed oil

Dip catfish fillets in Fish Batter. Shake off excess batter. Heat oil to 350°. Fry catfish fillets 4 to 6 minutes. For thicker fillets, fry 6 to 8 minutes.

CRAWFISH TAILS

Fresh crawfish tails   Water
Crabfinger Batter   Cottonseed oil
   (See page 30)

Dip crawfish tails in Crabfinger Batter, then water. Dip crawfish tails in Crabfinger Batter again before frying. Heat oil to 350°. Fry tails 3 to 5 minutes.

CRABFINGERS

Fresh crabfingers   Crabfinger Batter
Water   (See page 30)
           Cottonseed oil

Dip crabfingers in water then Crabfinger Batter. Repeat this step. Heat oil to 350°. Fry crabfingers 3 to 4 minutes.

SOFT-SHELLED CRAB

Fresh soft-shelled crabs   Crabfinger Batter
Water   (See page 30)
Self-rising flour   Cottonseed oil

Pull out eyes. Lift each side of crab and clean thoroughly. Dip soft-shelled crabs in water, then flour. Dip in water again, then in Crabfinger Batter. Heat oil to 350°. Fry soft-shell crabs 6 to 8 minutes.

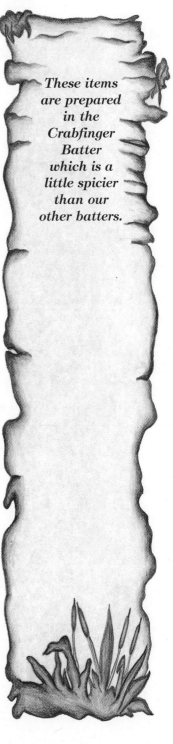

These items are prepared in the Crabfinger Batter which is a little spicier than our other batters.

ACE
(ALL-YOU-CAN-EAT WHOLE CATFISH)

Fresh whole catfish   Fish Batter (See page 30)
Water

Clean and skin whole catfish. Make 3 crosswise slits to the bone on each side of fish. Dip whole catfish in water then Fish Batter. Heat oil to 350°. Fry catfish 8 to 10 minutes.

In my opinion, the smaller the fish, the better. I always start off by eating the tail, then I tackle the rest of the fish with plenty of purple onions and ketchup.

72

SPECIALTIES

MIKE ANDERSON'S Seafood

Specialties

STUFFED FILLET OF FLOUNDER

3	cups chopped yellow onions	½	pound crabmeat (claw)
¾	cup chopped green bell peppers	½	pound white crabmeat (backfin)
1	teaspoon fresh minced garlic	3	tablespoons chopped green onions
1	stick margarine or butter	½	cup fresh bread crumbs
1½	teaspoons salt	4	pounds fresh fish fillets, thinly sliced lengthwise
¼	teaspoon cayenne pepper		
2	teaspoons black pepper	5	tablespoons butter, melted
1	pound fresh, peeled 90 to 110 count shrimp	1	teaspoon paprika
		1	teaspoon parsley flakes

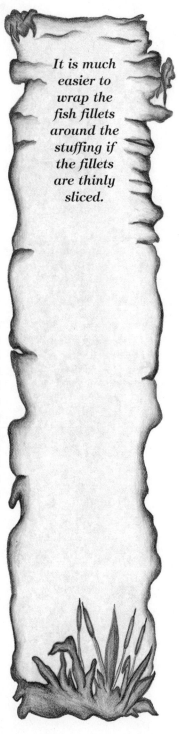

It is much easier to wrap the fish fillets around the stuffing if the fillets are thinly sliced.

In a medium saucepan, sauté yellow onions, bell peppers and garlic in margarine or butter. Cover and simmer 10 minutes over low heat. Add salt, cayenne pepper and black pepper. Stir. Add shrimp and all crabmeat. Simmer 8 minutes. Add green onions and bread crumbs. Stir. Mold 1 cup of stuffing into the shape of a dome. Wrap fish fillets around stuffing, starting at base of dome. Wrap until stuffing is completely covered with fish fillets. Pour butter into a shallow baking pan. Place stuffed fillets in pan. Cover with aluminum foil. Bake for 30 minutes at 450°. Remove foil and bake 3 to 4 more minutes to brown top. Baste each stuffed fillet with butter from bottom of pan. Garnish with paprika and parsley before serving.

Serves 6 to 8 people

MIKE'S SUPREME

This sauce can also be used as a marinade for crabfingers and other seafood, or as a steak topping. When serving this recipe, always stir sauce thoroughly because the onions and seasonings settle on bottom. I came up with this recipe in a very unique way. Late one night, I decided it was time to add to my menu of poyboys and gumbo. I gave the dishwasher a piece of paper and a pen, and told him to "Follow me and write down everything I pour in." After I added everything in reach, I tasted my creation. I, of course, thought it was "Supreme."

1 cup finely chopped yellow onions
3 tablespoons chicken base
¼ teaspoon hot sauce
2 tablespoons mustard
1 tablespoon plus 2 teaspoons ketchup
4 teaspoons black pepper
2 tablespoons plus 2 teaspoons garlic salt

Juice of ½ a lemon
2½ tablespoons Worcestershire sauce
⅔ cup cream sherry
2 sticks margarine or butter, melted
½ jumbo yellow onion, thinly sliced
1 pound fresh, peeled 16 to 20 count shrimp, butterflied

In a large bowl, combine chopped onions, chicken base, hot sauce, mustard, ketchup, black pepper, garlic salt, lemon juice, Worcestershire sauce and sherry. Stir. Pour margarine or butter into a shallow baking dish. Add contents of bowl, sliced onions and shrimp. Broil on high 4 minutes and stir. Broil another 4 minutes or until shrimp are done. Serve with garlic bread.

Serves 4 to 6 people

MIKE'S SPECIAL

5	sticks margarine or butter, melted	1	teaspoon cayenne pepper
4	teaspoons black pepper	3	cups Worcestershire sauce
5	teaspoons minced garlic	1	pound fresh peeled 16 to 20 count shrimp, butterflied

In a large bowl, combine margarine or butter, black pepper, granulated garlic, cayenne pepper and Worcestershire sauce. Stir. Pour into a shallow baking dish. Add shrimp. Broil on high 4 minutes. Stir. Broil another 4 minutes or until shrimp are done. Serve with garlic bread.

Serves 4 to 6 people

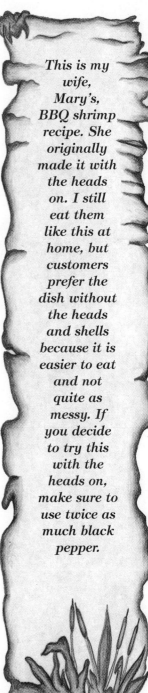

This is my wife, Mary's, BBQ shrimp recipe. She originally made it with the heads on. I still eat them like this at home, but customers prefer the dish without the heads and shells because it is easier to eat and not quite as messy. If you decide to try this with the heads on, make sure to use twice as much black pepper.

GUITREAU

9	cups chopped yellow onions	1½	pounds fresh, peeled 90 to 110 count shrimp
8	sticks butter or margarine, melted, divided	1½	pounds crawfish tails
2½	teaspoons salt	30	button mushrooms
¼	cup granulated garlic	½	cup chopped green onions
¾	teaspoon white pepper	6-8	(8-ounce) fresh fish fillets
½	teaspoon paprika	¼	cup dry white wine

In a large saucepan, sauté yellow onions in 3 sticks butter or margarine. Cover and simmer 20 to 30 minutes over low heat. Stir frequently. Add salt, garlic and white pepper. Add remaining 5 sticks butter or margarine, wine, and paprika. Cook over low heat until creamy. Add shrimp. Cook until shrimp are done. Add crawfish and mushrooms. Cook over low heat until hot. Add green onions before serving. Grill fish fillets until done. Spoon sauce over grilled fish fillets and serve.

Serves 6 to 8 people

If you're not in the mood to light up the grill, the fillets can be broiled in the oven. Just sprinkle with salt and pepper and broil on high in margarine or butter 8 to 10 minutes. The Guitreau sauce also makes a good steak and chicken topping. The Guitreau is named after Bo Guitreau, the famous Mike Anderson's Seafood repairman.

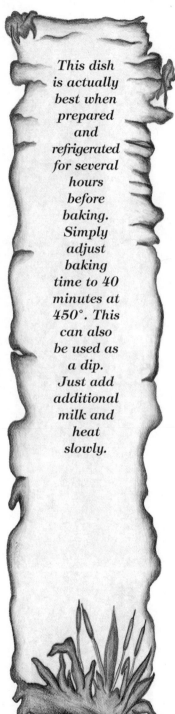

S·P·E·C·I·A·L·T·I·E·S

CRABMEAT AU GRATIN

4	cups chopped yellow onions	4	ounces mozzarella cheese, shredded
¾	cup chopped celery	6	cups evaporated milk, divided
1	stick butter or margarine	2	egg yolks
1¼	teaspoons salt	2	tablespoons chopped green onions
½	teaspoon cayenne pepper	1	pound white crabmeat (lump)
½	cup self-rising flour	1	pound crabmeat (claw)
4	ounces American cheese, shredded		

In a large saucepan, sauté yellow onions and celery in butter or margarine. Cover and simmer 15 to 20 minutes over low heat. Add salt and cayenne pepper. Stir. Add flour, American cheese and mozzarella cheese. Cook over medium heat until cheese melts. Add 3 cups evaporated milk. Stir. In a separate bowl, mix egg yolks with remaining 3 cups milk. Gradually add egg yolk mixture to saucepan. Cook over low heat until creamy. Add green onions and all crabmeat. Spoon into a casserole dish. Bake 20 minutes at 450°. Serve immediately.

Serves 6 to 8 people

This dish is actually best when prepared and refrigerated for several hours before baking. Simply adjust baking time to 40 minutes at 450°. This can also be used as a dip. Just add additional milk and heat slowly.

JOLIET ROUGE

Try this topping on a steak or just by itself. The Joliet Rouge received its name years ago from Jody Vernon. She was the winner of the contest I held asking the waitstaff to suggest a name for this new dish. Joliet Rouge is French for "pretty red".

9   cups chopped yellow onions
8   sticks butter or margarine, melted, divided
2   teaspoons salt
¼   cup granulated garlic
¾   teaspoon white pepper

30   button mushrooms
1   pound white crabmeat (lump)
½   cup chopped green onions
6-8   (8-ounce) fresh fish fillets

In a medium saucepan, sauté yellow onions in 3 sticks butter or margarine. Cover and simmer 15 to 20 minutes over low heat. Stir frequently. Add salt, garlic and white pepper. Stir. Add remaining 5 sticks butter or margarine. Add mushrooms, crabmeat and green onions. Simmer over medium heat until creamy. Broil fish fillets on high 8 to 10 minutes. Top broiled fish fillets with sauce and serve.

Serves 6 to 8 people

CRAWFISH AND CRABMEAT OVER FETTUCCINI

4 cups chopped yellow onions	½ cup self-rising flour
¾ cup chopped celery	4 ounces American cheese, shredded
1 stick butter or margarine	4 ounces mozzarella cheese, shredded
1¼ teaspoons salt	6 cups evaporated milk
½ teaspoon cayenne pepper	2 egg yolks
1 teaspoon basil	1 pound white crabmeat (lump or backfin)
1 teaspoon granulated garlic	1 pound crawfish tails
¼ teaspoon crushed red pepper	2 tablespoons chopped green onions
½ cup diced Rotel tomatoes, drained	8 cups cooked fettuccini pasta

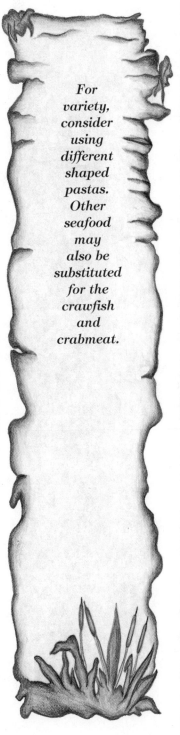

For variety, consider using different shaped pastas. Other seafood may also be substituted for the crawfish and crabmeat.

In a large saucepan, sauté yellow onions and celery in butter or margarine. Cover and simmer 15 to 20 minutes over low heat. Add salt, cayenne pepper, basil, granulated garlic, crushed red pepper and Rotel tomatoes. Stir. In a separate bowl, combine flour, American cheese, mozzarella cheese, evaporated milk and egg yolks. Stir well. Add milk mixture to saucepan. Stir. Add crabmeat and crawfish. Cook until creamy. Add green onions. Pour sauce over pasta and serve.

Serves 6 to 8 people

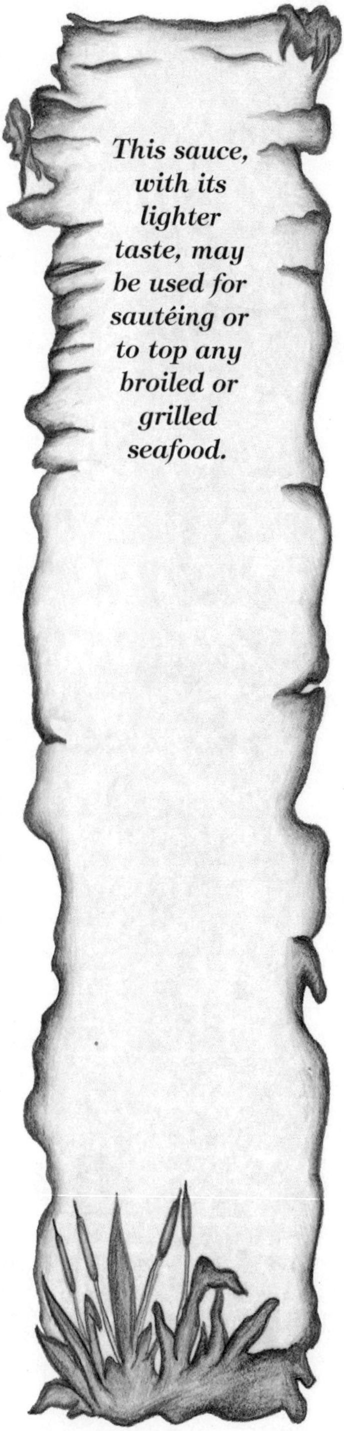

BROILED FILLET

SAUCE

2   sticks margarine or butter
1   tablespoon Mike Anderson's South Louisiana Seasoning or Season All
3   tablespoons fresh lemon juice

In a small saucepan, melt margarine. Add seasoning and fresh lemon juice. Cook over low heat 2 to 3 minutes.

Yield: 1 cup

BROILED FILLET

1   stick margarine or butter, melted
6-8 (12-ounce) fresh fish fillets
Salt
Pepper

Pour margarine or butter into a shallow baking pan. Place fish fillets in pan. Broil on high 10 to 12 minutes. Sprinkle with salt and pepper. Top each fish fillet with sauce and serve.

Serves 6 to 8 people

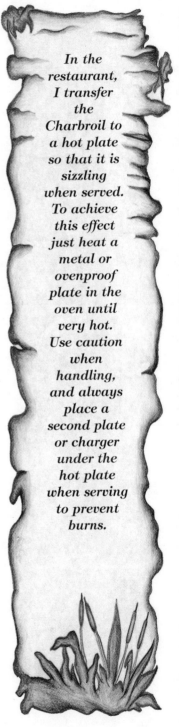

CHARBROIL

3	sticks margarine or butter, divided	1	bulb garlic, coarsely chopped
1	tablespoon Worcestershire sauce	1	teaspoon salt
1	tablespoon hot sauce	1	whole lemon, quartered
1¼	teaspoons black pepper	6-8	(12-ounce) fish fillets

In a small saucepan, melt 2 sticks margarine or butter. Add Worcestershire sauce, hot sauce, black pepper, garlic and salt. Stir. Squeeze lemon juice into saucepan, then drop lemon into pan as well. Sauté until garlic is tender. Set aside. Melt remaining 1 stick margarine or butter. Pour into a baking dish. Add fish fillets to baking dish and broil on high 10 to 12 minutes. Spoon 2 tablespoons of Charbroil sauce over each fish fillet making sure to include more chopped garlic than margarine in each spoonful.

Serves 6 to 8 people

In the restaurant, I transfer the Charbroil to a hot plate so that it is sizzling when served. To achieve this effect just heat a metal or ovenproof plate in the oven until very hot. Use caution when handling, and always place a second plate or charger under the hot plate when serving to prevent burns.

SNAPPER RUE BOURBON

*Be careful
not to
overcook.
As with
any cheese
based
sauce, low
heat should
be used,
and sauce
should be
served
immediately.*

2¾ cups chopped yellow onions
½ cup chopped green bell peppers
1 stick margarine or butter
1½ teaspoons salt
¼ teaspoon white pepper
¼ teaspoon cayenne pepper
¼ teaspoon thyme
⅓ cup Jack Daniel's (bourbon)
⅓ cup self-rising flour
6½ ounces American cheese, cubed
3¾ cups evaporated milk
1¼ pounds crawfish tails
6-8 (12-ounce) fresh fish fillets

In a medium saucepan, sauté onions and bell peppers in margarine or butter. Cover and simmer 15 to 20 minutes. Add salt, white pepper, cayenne pepper, thyme, bourbon and flour. Stir. Add cheese and milk. Cook over low heat while continuing to stir. Add crawfish tails. Cook until creamy. Broil fish fillets on high 10 to 12 minutes. Place fish on a serving platter and spoon Rue Bourbon sauce over fish fillets.

Serves 6 to 8 people

SHRIMP VICTORIA

5	cups chopped yellow onions	1	cup sour cream
⅔	cup chopped green bell peppers	⅓	cup white wine
1½	sticks margarine or butter	⅓	cup self-rising flour
		2	cups low-fat milk
2	teaspoons salt	½	pound fresh, peeled 90 to 110 count shrimp
1¼	teaspoons cayenne pepper	2½	cups fresh sliced mushrooms
¾	teaspoon white pepper	6-8	(12-ounce) fresh fish fillets
1¼	tablespoons Worcestershire sauce		

This has always been a customer favorite, as well as one of my own.

In a medium saucepan, sauté onions and bell peppers in margarine or butter. Cover and simmer over low heat 35 minutes. Stir frequently. Add salt, cayenne pepper, white pepper, Worcestershire sauce, sour cream, white wine and flour. Gradually add milk while continuing to stir. Simmer 8 minutes over low heat. Add shrimp. Cook until shrimp are done. Add sliced mushrooms. Set aside. Broil fish on high 10 to 12 minutes. Place fish on a serving platter and spoon Victoria sauce over fish fillets.

Serves 6 to 8 people

CRABMEAT MORNAY

I serve the Crabmeat Mornay both as a fish topping and as a casserole.

7 cups chopped yellow onions
1½ sticks butter or margarine
1 teaspoon salt
2 teaspoons white pepper
¼ cup self-rising flour

½ cup white wine
1 cup low-fat milk
1 cup half-and-half
1 pound white crabmeat (lump or backfin)
½ cup chopped green onions

In a medium saucepan, sauté yellow onions in butter or margarine. Cover and simmer over low heat 30 minutes. Stir frequently. Add salt, white pepper and flour. Stir. Add wine and milk. Gradually add half-and-half. Stir. Cook over low heat 8 to 10 minutes until creamy. Add crabmeat. Simmer until thoroughly hot. Add green onions. Stir. Pour Mornay Sauce into a casserole dish. Broil on high until top is golden brown.

Serves 6 to 8 people

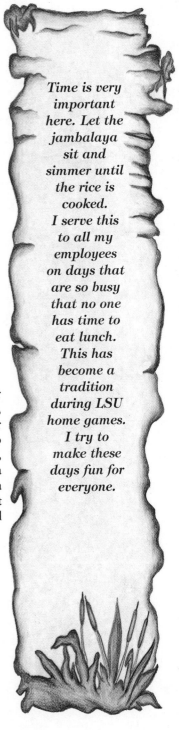

S·P·E·C·I·A·L·T·I·E·S

CHICKEN, SAUSAGE AND SEAFOOD JAMBALAYA

1	pound boneless, skinless chicken strips	2	tablespoons Worcestershire sauce
1½	pounds smoked sausage, sliced	½	tablespoon salt
1	cup cottonseed oil	2	teaspoons black pepper
6	cups chopped yellow onions	2½	tablespoons Mike Anderson's South Louisiana Seasoning or Season All
1¾	cups chopped green bell peppers		
¾	cup chopped celery	6	cups water
2	tablespoons fresh minced garlic	3¼	cups uncooked rice
3	(10-ounce) cans diced Rotel tomatoes	2	pounds fresh, peeled 90 to 110 count shrimp
1	(8-ounce) can tomato sauce	1	pound crabmeat (claw)
2	tablespoons fresh lemon juice	1	cup chopped green onions

In a cast iron pot, brown chicken and sausage in oil over high heat. Remove meat and set aside. Add yellow onions, bell peppers, celery and garlic to oil. Cover and simmer over low heat until tender. Add Rotel tomatoes and tomato sauce. Stir. Add lemon juice, Worcestershire sauce, salt, black pepper and Mike Anderson's South Louisiana Seasoning or Season All. Add water and rice. Bring to a boil. Add chicken and sausage to pot. Add shrimp, crabmeat and green onions. Cover and cook over medium heat until rice and shrimp are done.

Serves 6 to 8 people

Time is very important here. Let the jambalaya sit and simmer until the rice is cooked. I serve this to all my employees on days that are so busy that no one has time to eat lunch. This has become a tradition during LSU home games. I try to make these days fun for everyone.

SEAFOOD STUFFED BELL PEPPERS

These stuffed peppers are served on our Broiled Seafood Platters.

3-4	whole green bell peppers
¾	cup chopped yellow onions
¼	cup chopped celery
2	teaspoons fresh minced garlic
2	tablespoons plus 1 teaspoon margarine or butter
¾	teaspoon salt
½	teaspoon black pepper
½	cup condensed cream of mushroom soup
½	pound crawfish tails
½	cup cooked rice
2½	tablespoons chopped green onions
	Paprika
	Grated Parmesan cheese

Cut bell peppers in half. Remove seeds. Boil pepper halves until slightly tender. Drain. Set aside. In a medium saucepan, sauté yellow onions, celery and garlic in margarine or butter. Cover and simmer 15 to 20 minutes over low heat. Stir frequently. Add salt and pepper. Stir. Add mushroom soup and crawfish tails. Cook 8 minutes or until creamy. Add rice and green onions. Stir well. Fill each pepper half with stuffing. Sprinkle paprika and Parmesan cheese on top. Bake 20 minutes at 450°. Serve hot!

Serves 6 to 8 people

S·P·E·C·I·A·L·T·I·E·S

SHRIMP AND CRABMEAT AU GRATIN

1 pound 90 to 110 count shrimp, boiled and peeled	½ cup self-rising flour
1 cup fresh mushrooms	3 egg yolks
4½ cups chopped yellow onions	1 (12-ounce) can evaporated milk
2¼ cups chopped celery	8 ounces American cheese, cubed
6 tablespoons margarine or butter	8 ounces mozzarella cheese, shredded
1½ teaspoons salt	1 cup fresh mushrooms, sliced
½ teaspoon cayenne pepper	1 pound white crabmeat (lump)
2½ tablespoons granulated garlic	½ cup chopped green onions

Boil shrimp and mushrooms together 3 to 4 minutes. Drain. Finely chop mushrooms. Set aside. In a large saucepan, sauté yellow onions and celery in margarine or butter. Cover and simmer 20 to 30 minutes over low heat. Add salt, cayenne pepper, garlic and flour. Stir. In a separate bowl, mix egg yolks and milk. Add egg yolk mixture to saucepan. Add both cheeses. Add boiled shrimp and chopped mushrooms that have been set aside. Add sliced mushrooms and crabmeat. Stir. Cook until creamy. Add green onions. Spoon into a casserole dish. Bake 20 minutes at 450°. Serve immediately.

Serves 6 to 8 people

This dish is actually best when prepared and refrigerated for several hours before baking. If refrigerated, simply adjust baking time to 40 minutes at 450°. This also can be used as a dip. Just add additional milk and heat slowly.

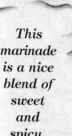

S·P·E·C·I·A·L·T·I·E·S

MARINATED CHICKEN BREASTS

This marinade is a nice blend of sweet and spicy.

1½ teaspoons black
    pepper
1½ tablespoons
    granulated garlic
1   tablespoon hot sauce

2   tablespoons
    Tiger Sauce*
½   cup brown sugar
4-5 boneless, skinless
    chicken breasts

Mix all ingredients except chicken in a bowl. Add chicken breasts and marinate over night. Grill and serve.

Yield: 1 cup marinade, serves 4 to 5 people

**If you have difficulty finding Tiger Sauce,
try www.tigersauce.com.*

The Howard

Howard Sauce

1¼ cups olive oil
⅔ cup fresh lemon juice
½ tablespoon parsley flakes
¼ cup Worcestershire sauce
1½ tablespoons crushed red pepper
1½ tablespoons salt
2½ tablespoons Mike Anderson's South Louisiana Seasoning or Season All
2½ tablespoons fresh minced garlic

Mix all ingredients together. Marinate fish over night in some of the sauce, reserving some for spooning over fish before serving.

Baked Fillet

1 stick margarine or butter, melted
6-8 (16-ounce) fresh fish fillets (skin and scales left on)
Salt
Pepper

Pour margarine or butter into a baking dish. Remove fish from marinade, reserving marinade. Place fish fillets in baking dish (skin-side down). Sprinkle with salt and pepper. Spoon 2 tablespoons of marinade on top of each fish fillet. Bake 30 minutes at 450°. Spoon reserved Howard sauce (not used for marinade) on top of each fish fillet before serving.

Yield: 1 cup sauce, serves 6 to 8 people

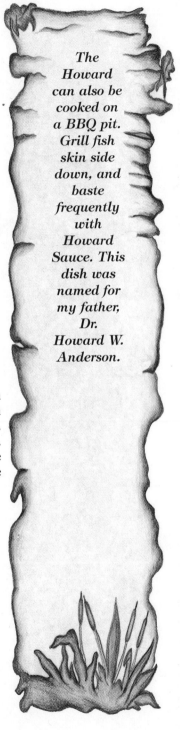

The Howard can also be cooked on a BBQ pit. Grill fish skin side down, and baste frequently with Howard Sauce. This dish was named for my father, Dr. Howard W. Anderson.

ITALIAN STUFFED SHRIMP

1½ cups chopped yellow onions	½ pound white crabmeat (backfin)
¼ cup chopped green bell peppers	2 teaspoons parsley flakes
¼ cup chopped celery	2½ tablespoons chopped green onions
½ teaspoon fresh minced garlic	¾ cup fresh Italian bread crumbs, divided
2 sticks margarine or butter, melted, divided	3 tablespoons water
½ teaspoon salt	½ cup grated Parmesan cheese
¼ teaspoon cayenne pepper	1 pound fresh, peeled 31 to 35 count shrimp, butterflied
1¼ teaspoons fresh lemon juice	Cottonseed oil
1¼ teaspoons Worcestershire sauce	Water
	Flour

Using a medium saucepan, sauté yellow onions, bell peppers, celery and garlic in 1 stick margarine or butter. Cover and simmer 20 minutes over low heat. Stir frequently. Add salt, cayenne pepper, lemon juice and Worcestershire sauce. Stir. Simmer 12 minutes over low heat. Add crabmeat, parsley and green onions. Stir. Gradually add ½ cup of bread crumbs while continuing to stir. Add 3 tablespoons water, remaining bread crumbs and Parmesan cheese. Stir. Mold stuffing around shrimp. To fry stuffed shrimp, heat cottonseed oil to 350°. Dip stuffed shrimp in water, then flour. Repeat this step. Fry in hot oil 8 minutes. Drain. Place fried stuffed shrimp in a casserole dish in remaining 1 stick margarine or butter. Sprinkle Parmesan cheese on top of shrimp. Bake 2 to 3 minutes at 450°. Serve immediately.

Serves 6 to 8 people

STUFFED CHICKEN BREASTS

2½ cups chopped yellow onions
¾ cup chopped green bell peppers
⅓ cup chopped celery
½ teaspoon minced garlic
4 tablespoons margarine or butter
1¼ teaspoon salt
½ teaspoon cayenne pepper
¾ pound crabmeat (claw)
2 teaspoons parsley flakes

2¾ tablespoons chopped green onions
¼ cup fresh bread crumbs
6-8 skinless, boneless chicken breasts, butterflied and tenderized
Paprika
Mike Anderson's South Louisiana Seasoning or Season All
Butter, melted

We serve this as a lunch special on Mondays at our Baton Rouge location.

In a small saucepan, sauté yellow onions, bell peppers, celery and garlic in margarine or butter. Cover and simmer 20 to 30 minutes over low heat. Stir frequently. Add salt and cayenne pepper. Stir. Add crabmeat. Cook 4 to 5 minutes over low heat. Add parsley and green onions. Stir. Gradually add bread crumbs. Stir. Spoon ½ cup of stuffing onto the center of each chicken breast and roll up. Place stuffed chicken breasts in a baking dish and cover with aluminum foil. Bake 30 minutes at 450°. Uncover dish and bake for 3 to 4 more minutes. Sprinkle paprika and Mike Anderson's South Louisiana Seasoning or Season All on top of each breast. Lightly brush each stuffed chicken breast with butter before serving.

Serves 6 to 8 people

SHRIMP AND CRABMEAT PASTA ALFREDO

"Big Al," who works at the Bourbon Street location of Mike Anderson's Seafood, gave me this recipe.

½	pound fresh, peeled 90 to 110 count shrimp	7	cups grated Parmesan cheese
2	sticks butter or margarine	3½	pounds crabmeat (claw)
6	cups heavy cream	½	cup chopped green onions
1½	teaspoons Mike Anderson's South Louisiana Seasoning or Season All	12	cups cooked fettuccini pasta

In a large saucepan, sauté shrimp in butter or margarine 2 to 4 minutes over low heat. Add cream, Mike Anderson's South Louisiana Seasoning or Season All and Parmesan cheese. Stir frequently. Simmer over low heat until creamy. Add crabmeat and green onions. Spoon over fettuccini pasta and serve.

Serves 6 to 8 people

CRAWFISH AU GRATIN

4	cups chopped yellow onions		4	ounces American cheese, shredded
¾	cup chopped celery		4	ounces mozzarella cheese, shredded
1	stick butter or margarine		6	cups evaporated milk, divided
1¼	teaspoons salt		2	egg yolks
½	teaspoon cayenne pepper		2	tablespoons chopped green onions
½	cup self-rising flour		1½	pounds crawfish tails

In a large saucepan, sauté yellow onions and celery in butter or margarine. Cover and simmer 15 to 20 minutes over low heat. Add salt and cayenne pepper. Stir. Add flour, American cheese and mozzarella cheese. Cook over medium heat until cheese melts. Add 3 cups evaporated milk. Stir. In a separate bowl, mix egg yolks with remaining 3 cups milk. Gradually add egg yolk mixture to saucepan. Cook over low heat until creamy. Add green onions and crawfish. Mix well. Spoon into a casserole dish. Bake 20 minutes at 450°. Serve immediately.

Serves 6 to 8 people

This dish is actually best when prepared and refrigerated for several hours before baking. If refrigerated, simply adjust baking time to 40 minutes at 450°. This can also be used as a dip. Just add additional milk and heat slowly.

TUNA TRI-STAR

Take caution when grilling tuna. It tends to dry out easily. This particular dish is by far the best selling "off-menu" special that I serve in my restaurants.

9	cups chopped yellow onions	¾	cup fresh mushrooms, sliced
8	sticks butter or margarine, melted, divided	1½	pounds white crabmeat (lump)
2	teaspoons salt	½	pound crawfish tails
4	tablespoons granulated garlic	½	pound fresh, peeled 90 to 110 count shrimp
¾	teaspoon white pepper	¼	cup chopped green onions
		6-7	(8-ounce) tuna steaks

In a medium saucepan, sauté yellow onions in 3 sticks butter or margarine. Cover and simmer 15 to 20 minutes over low heat. Stir frequently. Add salt, garlic and white pepper. Stir. Add remaining 5 sticks butter or margarine. Add mushrooms, crabmeat, crawfish, shrimp and green onions. Simmer over medium heat until creamy. Grill tuna steaks 3 to 4 minutes on each side or broil on high 6 to 8 minutes. Top tuna with sauce and serve.

Serves 6 to 8 people

CHICKEN AND SHRIMP SUPREME

1	cup finely chopped yellow onions
3	tablespoons chicken base
¼	teaspoon hot sauce
2	tablespoons mustard
1	tablespoon plus 2 teaspoons ketchup
4	teaspoons black pepper
2	tablespoons plus 2 teaspoons garlic salt

Juice of ½ a lemon
2½ tablespoons Worcestershire sauce

2	cups cream sherry
2	sticks margarine or butter, melted
2	pounds fresh, peeled 31 to 35 count shrimp, butterflied
6-8	cups cooked fettuccini pasta
2½	pounds skinless cooked chicken, cubed
½	jumbo onion, sliced
1	cup chopped green onions

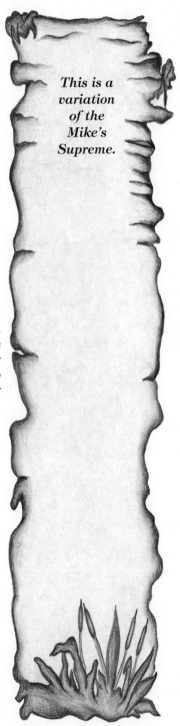

This is a variation of the Mike's Supreme.

Combine chopped onions, chicken base, hot sauce, mustard, ketchup, pepper, garlic salt, lemon juice, Worcestershire sauce and sherry in a large saucepan. Add margarine or butter and shrimp. Cook over medium heat until shrimp are done. Add pasta, chicken and sliced onions. Simmer until hot. Add green onions before serving.

Serves 6 to 8 people

COLLEGE TOWN REDFISH

This "off menu" special was named for my first restaurant.

6	(12-ounce) fresh redfish fillets	1½	sticks margarine or butter
⅓	cup Worcestershire sauce	1½	cups sliced fresh mushrooms
	Juice of one lemon	¼	cup chopped green onions
1	pound crabmeat (lump)		

Place redfish fillets in a baking dish. Top with Worcestershire sauce and freshly squeezed juice from one lemon. Broil on high 10 to 12 minutes. In a medium saucepan, sauté crabmeat and mushrooms in margarine or butter until hot. Add green onions. Spoon sauce over broiled fillets and serve.

Serves 6 to 8 people

THE ALLANTE

STUFFING

2½	cups chopped yellow onions	¾	pound crabmeat (claw)
¾	cup chopped green bell peppers	2	teaspoons parsley flakes
⅓	cup chopped celery	3	tablespoons chopped green onions
½	teaspoon minced garlic	¼	cup fresh bread crumbs
4	tablespoons margarine and butter	12	thin fresh fish fillets
1¼	teaspoons salt		Salt
½	teaspoon cayenne pepper		Pepper

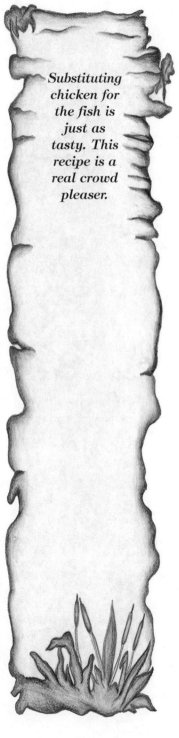

Substituting chicken for the fish is just as tasty. This recipe is a real crowd pleaser.

In a small saucepan, sauté yellow onions, bell peppers, celery and garlic in margarine or butter. Cover and simmer 20 to 30 minutes over low heat. Stir frequently. Add salt, cayenne pepper and crabmeat. Stir. Simmer until hot. Add parsley, green onions and bread crumbs. Stir. Spoon stuffing between 2 fish fillets. Repeat this step until all fillets are used. Sprinkle salt and pepper over fish. Broil on high 10 to 12 minutes.

TOPPING

8	sticks butter or margarine, divided	1½	pounds fresh, peeled 90 to 110 count shrimp
9	cups chopped yellow onions	1½	pounds crawfish tails
2½	teaspoons salt	30	button mushrooms
¼	cup granulated garlic	½	cup chopped green onions
¾	teaspoon white pepper		
½	teaspoon paprika		

In a large saucepan, sauté yellow onions in 3 sticks butter or margarine. Cover and simmer 20 to 30 minutes over low heat. Stir frequently. Add salt, granulated garlic and white pepper. Stir. Add remaining 5 sticks butter or margarine and paprika. Simmer over low heat until creamy. Add shrimp. Cook until shrimp are done. Add crawfish and mushrooms. Cook over low heat until hot. Add green onions before serving. Spoon topping over each stuffed fillet and serve.

Serves 6 to 8 people

WHOLE STUFFED FLOUNDER

This dish requires a little extra effort, but is well worth it. There is nothing like fresh flounder!

CRAB STUFFING

2½ cups chopped yellow onions	½ teaspoon cayenne pepper
¾ cup chopped green bell peppers	¾ pound crabmeat (claw)
⅓ cup chopped celery	2 teaspoons parsley flakes
½ teaspoon minced garlic	
4 tablespoons margarine or butter	3 tablespoons chopped green onions
1¼ teaspoons salt	¼ cup fresh bread crumbs

In a small saucepan, sauté yellow onions, bell peppers, celery and garlic in margarine or butter. Cover and simmer 20 to 30 minutes over low heat. Stir frequently. Add salt and cayenne pepper. Stir. Add crabmeat. Simmer until hot. Add parsley and green onions. Gradually add bread crumbs. Stir.

BUTTER TOPPING

2 sticks butter or margarine	2 tablespoons Mike Anderson's South Louisiana Seasoning or Season All
3 tablespoons fresh lemon juice	

In a small saucepan, melt butter or margarine. Add lemon juice and Mike Anderson's South Louisiana Seasoning or Season All. Simmer 2 to 3 minutes.

Yield: 1 cup

FLOUNDER

6-8 whole flounder	1 cup Butter Topping
2½ cups Crab Stuffing	¼ cup paprika
Salt	¼ cup parsley flakes
Pepper	

Scale and de-bone (book) flounder. Spoon Crab Stuffing into each de-boned flounder. Sprinkle salt and pepper on top of each stuffed flounder. Broil on high 12 to 15 minutes. Spoon Butter Topping on each fish. Top each stuffed flounder with paprika and parsley before serving.

Serves 6 to 8 people

THE PARMESAN

1½ sticks margarine or
    butter, melted
1½ cups white wine
6 (8-ounce) fresh fish
    fillets
1½ teaspoons salt
1½ teaspoons black
    pepper
1 tomato, thinly sliced

1 green bell pepper,
    thinly sliced
1 yellow onion, thinly
    sliced
1½ cups shredded
    Parmesan cheese
Paprika
Parsley flakes

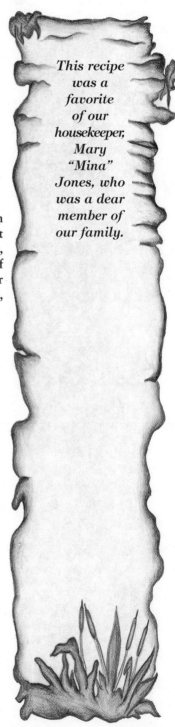

This recipe was a favorite of our housekeeper, Mary "Mina" Jones, who was a dear member of our family.

Pour margarine or butter and white wine into a medium baking dish. Place fish fillets in baking dish. Sprinkle salt and pepper on top of each fish fillet. Add sliced tomato, bell pepper and onion. Sprinkle Parmesan cheese on top of fish. Cover dish and bake 30 to 40 minutes at 450°. Uncover and sprinkle paprika and parsley on fish. Bake, uncovered, 2 minutes at 450°. Serve immediately.

Serves 6 people

PASTA PRIMAVERA

¼	pound crawfish tails	2	teaspoons salt
¼	pound fresh, peeled 90 to 110 count shrimp	1	teaspoon crushed red pepper
1	cup olive oil	1	tomato, diced
1	broccoli head, cut into florets	2	teaspoons crushed basil
1	purple onion, sliced	1	cup grated Parmesan cheese, divided
2	cups fresh sliced mushrooms	5	cups cooked rotini pasta
4	teaspoons finely chopped fresh garlic		

Sauté crawfish and shrimp in olive oil. Cook 1 minute over medium heat. Add broccoli, onion slices and mushrooms together. Stir. Add garlic, salt, crushed red pepper, tomatoes, basil, ½ cup Parmesan cheese and cooked pasta. Stir. Cook until shrimp are done. Top with remaining Parmesan cheese before serving.

Serves 4 people

THE DIABLO

2	cups BBQ Sauce (See page 27)	½	cup jalapeño slices, drained
2	sticks margarine or butter, melted	1	purple onion, thinly sliced
6-8	(8-ounce) fresh fish fillets	1	pound mozzarella cheese, shredded
1½	teaspoons salt	1	pound American cheese, shredded
1½	teaspoons black pepper	¾	cup parsley flakes

Pour BBQ sauce and margarine or butter into a baking dish. Place fish into baking dish. Sprinkle salt and pepper on fish. Top fish with jalapeños and purple onion slices. Broil on high 8 to 10 minutes. Sprinkle mozzarella and American cheese on top of fish. Broil on high another 2 minutes to melt cheese. Top with parsley and serve.

Serves 6 to 8 people

CRAWFISH SCAMPI

¾ cup coarsely chopped
    garlic
2 sticks margarine or
    butter
1½ tablespoons
    Worcestershire sauce
1 tablespoon hot sauce
1¼ teaspoons black
    pepper

Juice of 1½ lemons
1 teaspoon salt
1 tablespoon Mike
    Anderson's South
    Louisiana Seasoning
    or Season All
1 pound crawfish tails

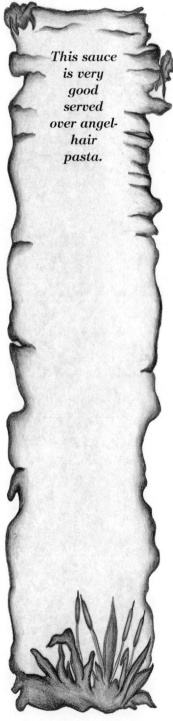

This sauce is very good served over angel-hair pasta.

In a small saucepan, sauté garlic in margarine or butter. Simmer over low heat until garlic is golden brown. Add Worcestershire sauce, hot sauce, black pepper, lemon juice, salt and Mike Anderson's South Louisiana Seasoning or Season All. Mix well. Pour scampi sauce into a shallow baking dish. Add crawfish tails. Bake 40 minutes at 450°, stirring often.

Serves 4 people

STUFFED CRABS

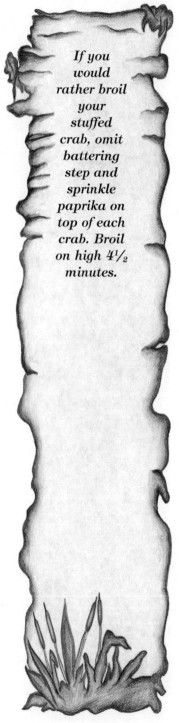

If you would rather broil your stuffed crab, omit battering step and sprinkle paprika on top of each crab. Broil on high 4¹⁄₂ minutes.

2½ cups chopped yellow onions	¾ pound crabmeat (claw)
¾ cup chopped green bell peppers	2 teaspoons parsley
⅓ cup chopped celery	2 tablespoons chopped green onions
1 teaspoon fresh minced garlic	2 cups fresh bread crumbs
5 tablespoons margarine or butter	6-8 cleaned crab shells
1 teaspoon salt	Self-rising flour
¼ teaspoon cayenne pepper	Crabfinger Batter (See page 30)
	Cottonseed oil

In a small saucepan, sauté yellow onions, bell peppers, celery and garlic in margarine or butter. Cover and simmer 20 to 30 minutes. Stir frequently. Add salt and cayenne pepper. Stir. Add crabmeat. Cook until hot. Add parsley and green onions. Gradually add bread crumbs. Stir. Spoon stuffing into crab shells. Firmly pack. Dip each stuffed crab in water then flour. Dip in water again, then Crabfinger Batter. Heat cottonseed oil to 350°. Fry 8 to 10 minutes. Drain and serve.

Serves 6 to 8 people

EGGPLANT PIROGUE

3	medium eggplants	1	tablespoon Worcestershire sauce	
5	cups chopped yellow onions	1¼	pounds crawfish tails	
3	cups chopped green bell peppers	1½	pounds fresh, peeled 90 to 110 count shrimp	
1	tablespoon fresh minced garlic	2	tablespoons fresh Italian bread crumbs	
1	stick margarine or butter		Crabfinger Batter (See page 30)	
1¼	tablespoons salt		Cottonseed oil	
¾	teaspoon cayenne pepper		Parmesan cheese	

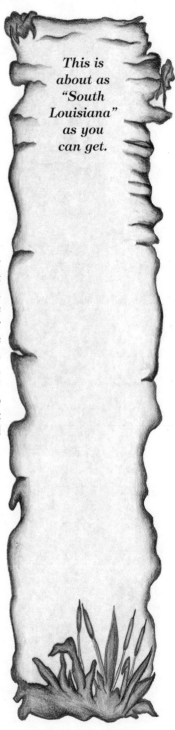

This is about as "South Louisiana" as you can get.

Peel eggplants and cut in half lengthwise. Scoop out center of eggplant, chop and set aside. The hollowed eggplant creates a "pirogue" to hold the stuffing. In a medium saucepan, sauté onions, bell peppers and garlic in margarine or butter. Cover and simmer 30 minutes over low heat. Stir frequently. Add salt, cayenne pepper and Worcestershire sauce. Add chopped eggplant, crawfish and shrimp. Stir. Simmer 8 minutes over low heat. Add bread crumbs. Stir. Heat cottonseed oil to 350°. Dip each eggplant "pirogue" in water then Crabfinger Batter. Repeat this step. Fry 6 to 8 minutes. Drain. Spoon eggplant stuffing into eggplant "pirogue." Sprinkle Parmesan cheese on top of each stuffed eggplant.

Serves 6 people

SEAFOOD STUFFED SHRIMP

As an alternative to frying, broil shrimp on high 6 to 8 minutes. Omit steps involving water, flour and batter. Top with paprika and Parmesan cheese and serve.

1½ cups chopped yellow onions
⅓ cup chopped green bell peppers
¼ cup chopped celery
½ teaspoon fresh minced garlic
5 tablespoons margarine or butter
½ teaspoon salt
¼ teaspoon cayenne pepper
1¼ teaspoons fresh lemon juice
1¼ teaspoons Worcestershire sauce
½ pound white crabmeat (backfin)
2¼ teaspoons parsley flakes
2 tablespoons chopped green onions
1¾ tablespoons fresh Italian bread crumbs
1 pound fresh, peeled 90 to 110 count shrimp, butterflied
Water
Self-rising flour
Fish batter (See page 30)
Cottonseed oil

In a medium saucepan, sauté yellow onions, bell peppers, celery and garlic in margarine or butter. Cover and simmer 20 minutes over low heat. Stir frequently. Add salt, cayenne pepper, lemon juice and Worcestershire sauce. Stir. Simmer 12 minutes over low heat. Add crabmeat, parsley, green onions and bread crumbs. Mold stuffing around each shrimp. Dip each stuffed shrimp in water then flour. Dip in water again, then Fish Batter. Heat cottonseed oil to 350°. Fry stuffed shrimp 6 to 8 minutes. Drain. Serve immediately.

Serves 6 to 8 people

TROUT NORMAN

TROUT

6-8 (8-ounce) fresh trout fillets
Self-rising flour
Cottonseed oil
Norman Sauce
Parsley flakes

Dip each fish fillet in water, then flour. Repeat this step. Heat cottonseed oil to 350°. Fry fish fillets 6 to 8 minutes. Drain. Place fried fish fillets on serving dish and top with Norman Sauce. Sprinkle parsley on top.

NORMAN SAUCE

6 cups chopped yellow onions
¾ cup chopped green bell peppers
½ cup chopped celery
2½ teaspoons fresh minced garlic
4 tablespoons butter
4 tablespoons margarine
2½ teaspoons salt
½ teaspoon cayenne pepper
1¾ cups light roux (See page 29)
4 cups water, divided
1½ pounds white crabmeat (lump or backfin), divided

In a medium pot, sauté onions, bell peppers, celery and garlic in butter and margarine. Cover and simmer 30 minutes over low heat. Stir frequently. Add salt, cayenne pepper and light roux. Stir. Simmer 5 to 7 minutes over medium heat. Add ½ cup water. Bring to a boil. Add remaining 3½ cups water and 1 pound of crabmeat. Stir. Bring to a boil. Add remaining crabmeat. Simmer over low heat until ready to serve.

Serves 6 to 8 people

This sauce is actually our Crabmeat Étouffée found on page 54. It is called Norman Sauce here because it tops our Trout Norman and our Shrimp Norman on page 108.

SHRIMP NORMAN

Try this on fried soft-shelled crabs.

SHRIMP

1 pound fresh peeled 16 to 20 count shrimp, butterflied	Cottonseed oil
	Norman Sauce
	Parsley flakes
Self-rising flour	

Dip each shrimp in water then flour. Repeat this step. Heat cottonseed oil to 350°. Using your hand, flatten butterflied shrimp. Fan layers at tip of tail. Drop flat into hot grease, causing shrimp to curl. Fry shrimp 4 to 6 minutes. Drain. Arrange shrimp pointing tails outward on a serving dish. Top with Norman Sauce. Sprinkle parsley on top.

Serves 6 to 8 people

NORMAN SAUCE

6 cups chopped yellow onions	2½ teaspoons salt
¾ cup chopped green bell peppers	½ teaspoon cayenne pepper
½ cup chopped celery	1¾ cups light roux (See page 29)
2½ teaspoons fresh minced garlic	4 cups water, divided
4 tablespoons butter	1½ pounds white crabmeat (lump or backfin), divided
4 tablespoons margarine	

In a medium pot, sauté onions, bell peppers, celery and garlic in butter and margarine. Cover and simmer 30 minutes over low heat. Stir frequently. Add salt, cayenne pepper and light roux. Stir. Simmer 5 to 7 minutes over medium heat. Add ½ cup water. Bring to a boil. Add remaining 3½ cups water and 1 pound of crabmeat. Stir. Bring to a boil. Add remaining crabmeat. Simmer over low heat until ready to serve.

Serves 6 to 8 people

THE LEFETE

12 cups chopped yellow onions
1 cup chopped green bell peppers
¾ cup chopped celery
2 teaspoons fresh minced garlic
1 stick margarine or butter
1½ tablespoons seafood stock (See page 28)
1¼ tablespoons salt
1½ teaspoons black pepper
1¼ cups light roux (See page 29)

1 (10-ounce) can diced Rotel tomatoes, drained
1 teaspoon granulated garlic
3¾ cups water
1 pound crawfish tails
2 tablespoons parsley flakes
6-8 (6-ounce) fresh fish fillets
Flour
Cottonseed oil
Parsley flakes

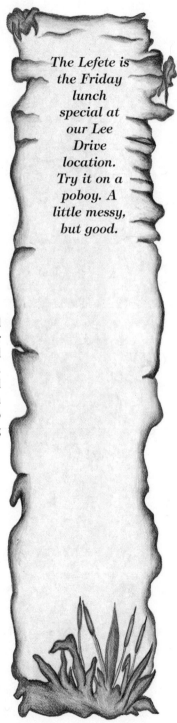

The Lefete is the Friday lunch special at our Lee Drive location. Try it on a poboy. A little messy, but good.

In a medium pot, sauté onions, bell peppers, celery and garlic in margarine or butter. Add seafood stock. Cover and simmer 45 minutes over low heat. Stir frequently. Add salt, pepper, roux, Rotel tomatoes, garlic and 3¾ cups water. Bring to a boil. Stir constantly. Add crawfish tails and parsley. Simmer 15 minutes. Stir well. Dip each fish fillet in water then flour. Repeat this step. Heat cottonseed oil to 350°. Fry fish fillets 6 to 8 minutes. Drain. Spoon topping mixture over each fish fillet. Top with parsley.

Serves 6 to 8 people

THE JASON

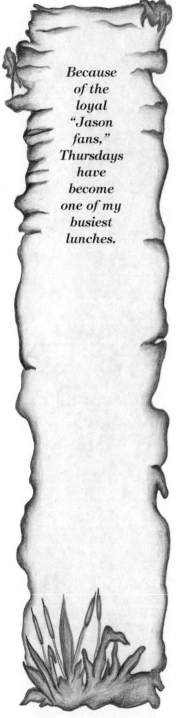

JASON SAUCE

3	cups chopped yellow onions	3	tablespoons self-rising flour
5	tablespoons margarine or butter	½	cup half-and-half
1	teaspoon salt	½	pound crawfish tails
⅛	teaspoon black pepper	1½	cups low-fat milk
¼	teaspoon cayenne pepper	½	cup chopped green onions

In a medium saucepan, sauté yellow onions in margarine or butter. Cover and simmer 30 minutes over low heat. Add salt, black pepper and cayenne pepper. Stir. Add flour, half-and-half, crawfish and milk while continuing to stir. Add green onions before serving.

JASON STUFFING

2½	cups chopped yellow onions	2	teaspoons parsley flakes
¾	cup chopped green bell peppers	2	tablespoons chopped green onions
⅓	cup chopped celery	2	cups fresh bread crumbs
1	teaspoon fresh minced garlic	6-8	fresh fish fillets, thinly sliced
5	tablespoons margarine or butter		Crabfinger Batter (See page 30)
1	teaspoon salt		Cottonseed oil
¼	teaspoon cayenne pepper	6	cups cooked rice
¾	pound crabmeat (claw)		

In a small saucepan, sauté yellow onions, bell peppers, celery and minced garlic in margarine or butter. Cover and simmer 20 to 30 minutes. Stir frequently. Add salt and cayenne pepper. Stir. Add crabmeat. Cook until hot. Add parsley and green onions. Gradually add bread crumbs. Stir. Spoon stuffing onto each fish fillet. Roll up. Dip in water then Crabfinger Batter. Repeat this step. Heat cottonseed oil to 350°. Fry until golden brown. Place fried stuffed fish fillets on a bed of rice. Top with Jason sauce.

Serves 6 to 8 people

SALADS

Mike Anderson's Seafood

Salads

HOUSE SALAD

HOUSE DRESSING

½	cup vegetable oil	½	teaspoon black pepper
⅓	cup water	3	tablespoons
¾	cup white vinegar		granulated garlic
2	tablespoons sugar	3	tablespoons grated
2	tablespoons fresh		Parmesan cheese
	minced garlic	¾	cup shredded Romano
2	tablespoons chopped		cheese
	green onions		

Mix all ingredients together. Chill.

Yield: 2 cups

HOUSE SALAD

1	head Romaine lettuce, torn	1	tomato, chopped
1	head iceberg lettuce, torn	1	purple onion, sliced
		½	cup House Dressing
		2	cups garlic croutons

Tear lettuce and put in a large mixing bowl. Add tomatoes, onions and House Dressing. Toss salad well. Before serving, top with croutons.

Serves 6 to 8 people

TAKE CAUTION: This dressing stays with you long after you are done eating. I suggest keeping a few mints in your pocket for the rest of the day.

COLESLAW

In the restaurant, there is a timer that sits next to the coleslaw. Every 15 minutes new coleslaw is made. This ensures that customers receive only the freshest, best-tasting coleslaw.

COLESLAW DRESSING

1	tablespoon fresh, finely minced garlic	3½	tablespoons sugar
1¼	cups mayonnaise	1	tablespoon black pepper
⅓	cup yellow mustard		

In a mixing bowl combine all ingredients. Stir well and refrigerate.

Yield: 2 cups

COLESLAW

15	cups shredded green cabbage	¾	cup finely chopped green bell peppers
2	cups shredded purple cabbage	2	tablespoons chopped green onions
1½	cups finely chopped yellow onions	2	cups Coleslaw Dressing

In a large mixing bowl, combine green cabbage, purple cabbage, onions, bell peppers and green onions. Using hands, toss well. Add Coleslaw Dressing. Toss and serve.

Serves 12 to 15 people

BLUE CHEESE DRESSING

2	tablespoons buttermilk	½	cup mayonnaise
1½	teaspoons olive oil	¾	cup crumbled blue
½	teaspoon black pepper		cheese
¾	cup sour cream		

Mix all ingredients together. Chill and serve.

Yield: 2 cups

I enjoy using this recipe as a dip for vegetable or relish trays.

THOUSAND ISLAND DRESSING

2	boiled eggs, diced	¼	teaspoon Worcestershire sauce
3	tablespoons sour cream	2	tablespoons chopped green onions
⅔	cup ketchup	¼	teaspoon hot sauce
4	tablespoons sweet relish	½	cup mayonnaise
½	teaspoon prepared horseradish	¼	teaspoon salt
¼	cup chopped black olives	¼	teaspoon sugar
		¼	teaspoon granulated garlic

Combine all ingredients in a bowl. Stir well. Chill and serve.

Yield: 2 cups

Be sure not to omit the black olives. They are crucial to the overall flavor of this dressing.

SHRIMP RÉMOULADE

This is especially refreshing served on a warm summer evening.

2½ tablespoons parsley flakes, divided
2 tablespoons finely chopped celery
2 boiled eggs, finely chopped
2¼ teaspoons prepared horseradish
1¼ teaspoons Creole mustard
¾ teaspoon yellow mustard
3½ tablespoons ketchup
2 tablespoons chopped green onions
¼ teaspoon hot sauce

¼ teaspoon Worcestershire sauce
½ teaspoon sugar
¼ teaspoon granulated garlic
¼ teaspoon salt
¾ cup mayonnaise
1 head iceberg lettuce
1 head Romaine lettuce
3-4 pounds fresh, peeled 90 to 110 count shrimp, boiled (See page 123)
3-4 carrots, peeled and cut into sticks

In a large mixing bowl, combine 2 tablespoons parsley, celery, eggs, horseradish, mustards, ketchup, onions, hot sauce, Worcestershire sauce, sugar, garlic, salt and mayonnaise. Toss iceberg and romaine lettuce in a separate bowl. Pour desired amount of dressing on top. Place shrimp on top of dressing. Sprinkle remaining parsley on the top. Garnish with carrot sticks.

Yield: 2 cups dressing, serves 6 to 8 people

Caesar Salad Dressing

¼ cup skim milk
1 teaspoon granulated garlic
2½ tablespoons vegetable oil
1 tablespoon olive oil
1 teaspoon fresh lemon juice
1 egg yolk
1 teaspoon hot sauce
1 teaspoon Worcestershire sauce
⅛ teaspoon ground mustard
¼ teaspoon black pepper
1¼ tablespoons finely chopped fresh anchovies
⅓ cup grated Parmesan cheese
¾ cup mayonnaise
Croutons, crumbled

Mix all ingredients together except croutons. Chill and serve with croutons sprinkled over salad.

Yield: 2 cups

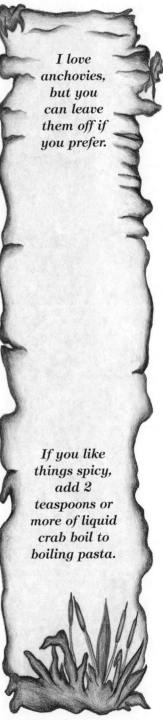

I love anchovies, but you can leave them off if you prefer.

Pasta Rotini Salad

6 cups cooked tri-colored rotini pasta
1 cup thinly sliced purple onion
½ pound white crabmeat (lump)
½ pound fresh, peeled 90 to 110 count shrimp, boiled and chopped (See page 123)
1 cup sliced black olives
1 teaspoon sugar
1 teaspoon grated Parmesan cheese
1 teaspoon salt

Drain pasta. In a large bowl, mix pasta, onions, crabmeat and shrimp. Add remaining ingredients. Stir. Chill and serve.

Serves 2 people

If you like things spicy, add 2 teaspoons or more of liquid crab boil to boiling pasta.

SHRIMP SALAD

May be stuffed in half an avocado or half a tomato for a cool treat on a hot Louisiana afternoon. This also makes good finger sandwiches. Simply chop the salad in a food processor.

2 cups chopped green bell peppers
1 cup chopped celery
1 cup thinly sliced purple onions
1½ cups chopped green onions
¾ teaspoon prepared horseradish
¾ teaspoon Worcestershire sauce
½ teaspoon hot sauce
⅛ teaspoon salt
⅛ teaspoon sugar

⅛ teaspoon granulated garlic
2 teaspoons black pepper
⅛ teaspoon fresh lemon juice
½ cup ketchup
½ cup mayonnaise
1½ teaspoons garlic salt
12 boiled eggs, diced
1½ pounds fresh, peeled 90 to 110 count shrimp, boiled (See page 123)

Combine all ingredients. Stir. Chill and serve on a bed of lettuce.

Serves 2 to 4 people

Boiled Seafood

CRAB BOIL

12	gallons water
6	cups salt
6	cups liquid crab boil
½	cup lemon juice
½	cup celery salt
⅓	cup granulated garlic

⅓	cup Mike Anderson's South Louisiana Seasoning or Season All
¾	cup fresh minced garlic
30	pounds fresh crabs

In a 15-gallon pot, add water and all ingredients except crabs. Cover and bring to a rolling boil (approximately 20 minutes). Add crabs and cover. Bring back to a rolling boil. Turn off heat immediately. Gently stir and soak crabs until they sink. (approximately 25 minutes). Drain and enjoy.

Yield: 30 pounds, 6 dozen

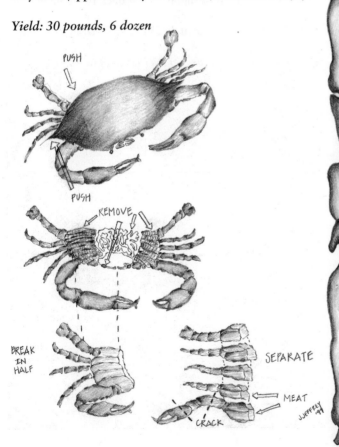

Eating boiled crabs takes patience. I recommend trying them on the Sideporch at Mike Anderson's Seafood Restaurant in Baton Rouge. Have a cold beer or a glass of iced tea with your crabs, and relax. All good things take time.

121

CRAWFISH BOIL

In South Louisiana, everyone has their own recipe and procedures for boiling crawfish, and they are all the best. I have found through the years that my customers have been most receptive to this particular recipe. There are numerous extras you can add to your crawfish boil. Among them, mushrooms, whole artichokes and, of course, the infamous corn and potatoes. My friends, Dr. Gayle Sanchez and Dr. Jimmie Hammack, insist that I include chicken pieces and sausage for their annual office crawfish boil. Always remember, at a crawfish boil, "Whoever eats the fastest gets the mostest!"

10 gallons water
7 cups salt
8 cups liquid crab boil
2 cups fresh lemon juice
1 cup celery salt
½ cup granulated garlic
½ cup Mike Anderson's South Louisiana Seasoning or Season All
1 cup fresh minced garlic
¾ cup cayenne pepper
35 pounds fresh crawfish (one sack)

In a 20-gallon pot, add all ingredients except crawfish. Cover and bring to a rolling boil (approximately 20 minutes). Add crawfish and stir thoroughly. Bring back to a rolling boil. Turn off heat immediately. Stir again and soak until all crawfish sink (approximately 25 minutes). Drain and enjoy.

Yield: 35 pounds, serves 10 average people or 3 true South Louisiana natives

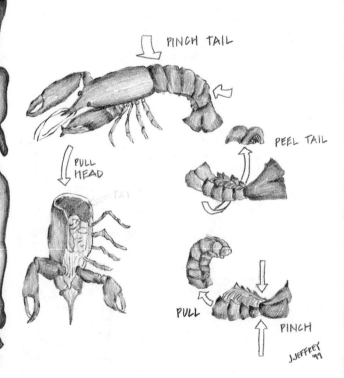

PINCH TAIL

PEEL TAIL

PULL HEAD

PULL

PINCH

J.JEFFREY '99

SHRIMP BOIL

2	gallons water	2	tablespoons granulated garlic
1¼	cups salt	⅓	cup cayenne pepper
1¼	cups liquid crab boil	10	pounds fresh 90 to 110 or 36 to 42 count shrimp
½	cup fresh lemon juice		
2	tablespoons celery salt		

In a 5-gallon pot, add all ingredients except shrimp. Cover and bring to a rolling boil (approximately 10 to 12 minutes). Add shrimp and bring back to a rolling boil. Turn off heat immediately. Stir well and soak shrimp until they sink. Drain and enjoy.

Yield: 10 pounds

SLINGER

Juice of 3 lemons		5	cups ice
1½	cups Sprite	¾	cup sugar
1	cup Absolute Citron		

Combine all ingredients in a blender. Blend 2 to 3 minutes or until sugar is dissolved.

Yield: 5 cups

There's nothing like hot shrimp out of the pot, but one of the greatest things about boiled shrimp is that they are just as good cold. However you choose to eat them, I highly recommend serving them with a batch of my signature drink, The Slinger.

SIDE DISHES

Side Dishes

ALLIGATOR SAUSAGE

2	pounds alligator meat	⅓	cup drained diced Rotel tomatoes
1	cup chopped yellow onions	½	teaspoon cayenne pepper
1	cup chopped green onions	¼	teaspoon white pepper
2	tablespoons fresh minced garlic	2	teaspoons salt
1	pound lean ground pork	2	teaspoons black pepper
			Sausage casings

Using a food processor, finely chop alligator meat. In a large bowl, combine chopped alligator meat and remaining ingredients except casings. Mix well. Fill casings. Boil sausages 5 to 10 minutes. Grill before serving.

Yield: 3 pounds

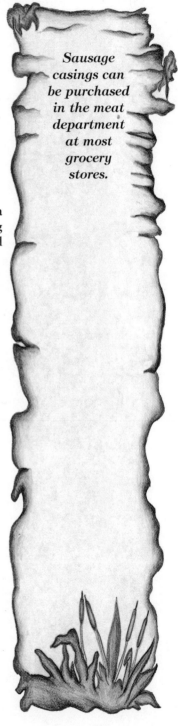

Sausage casings can be purchased in the meat department at most grocery stores.

ALLIGATOR BURGERS

I have found that a good spicy mustard (Dijon) or my BBQ Sauce complements this recipe.

2	pounds alligator meat	¼	teaspoon white pepper
1	cup chopped yellow onions	1	teaspoon salt
1	cup chopped green onions	2	teaspoons black pepper
2	tablespoons fresh minced garlic	1	pound lean ground pork
⅓	cup diced Rotel tomatoes, drained	1	egg
½	teaspoon cayenne pepper	1	cup fresh bread crumbs

Using a food processor, finely chop alligator meat. In a large bowl, add chopped alligator meat, yellow and green onions, garlic, Rotel tomatoes, cayenne pepper, white pepper, salt and black pepper. Mix well. Spoon mixture into a plastic bag. Seal bag. Place bag in boiling water 5 to 10 minutes. Carefully remove bag and open. Add boiled mixture to bowl. Stir. Add pork, egg and bread crumbs. Mix. Shape into patties. Grill or broil patties.

Yield: 3 pounds

STUFFED POTATOES

3 large potatoes, baked
½ pound bacon, cooked crisp and crumbled
¾ cup shredded cheddar cheese
1 teaspoon salt
1¼ teaspoons black pepper
1 tablespoon butter or margarine, melted
⅓ cup sour cream
1 cup low-fat milk
¼ cup chopped green onions

Cut each potato in half lengthwise. Scoop inside of potatoes into a large bowl, setting aside potato skins. Add remaining ingredients to bowl. Mix until creamy. Spoon mixture into reserved potato skins. Bake 20 to 30 minutes at 450°.

Serves 6 people

This recipe is actually best when prepared and refrigerated for several hours before baking. Bake 45 minutes to 1 hour at 450°. Consider eliminating potato skins and baking this recipe in a casserole dish for large groups.

HUSHPUPPIES

To achieve round hushpuppies, use a #70 scoop, which can be purchased at any specialty food store. Legend has it the name "hushpuppy" came about when an old Creole cook was frying a batch of catfish and croquettes. His hungry, hunting dogs began to howl for a chance to eat some catfish. The quick thinking Creole cook, instead, tossed a few croquettes to the dogs and yelled, "Hush, puppies!" The name has since been associated with this cornmeal delicacy.

1	tablespoon salt	½	cup finely chopped green bell peppers
2	teaspoons cayenne pepper	1½	cups finely chopped yellow onions
1½	cups sugar	2½	cups yellow cornmeal
½	teaspoon black pepper	1	cup self-rising flour
2	eggs		Cottonseed oil
1½	cups evaporated milk		
½	cup chopped green onions		

In a large bowl, combine all ingredients except oil. Mix well. Heat cottonseed oil to 350°. Drop hushpuppy mixture into hot oil by spoonfuls. Fry 4 to 6 minutes.

Serves 6 to 8 people

SOUTH LOUISIANA RICE

1	cup chopped yellow onions	2½	teaspoons Worcestershire sauce
1½	tablespoons fresh minced garlic	2½	teaspoons hot sauce
4	tablespoons butter or margarine	¼	cup toasted almonds
		2	tablespoons chopped pecans
1¼	teaspoons salt	4	cups cooked rice
1¼	teaspoons black pepper	1	tablespoon chopped green onions

In a small saucepan, sauté yellow onions and garlic in butter or margarine. Cover and simmer 15 minutes over low heat. Stir frequently. Add salt, black pepper, Worcestershire sauce and hot sauce. Stir well. Add almonds, pecans and rice. Stir. Add green onions before serving.

Serves 6 to 8 people

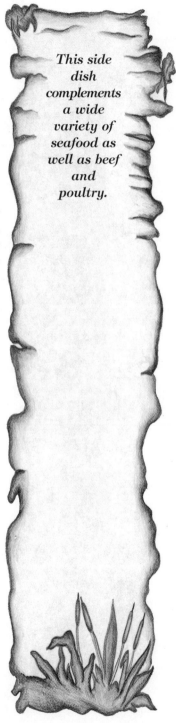

This side dish complements a wide variety of seafood as well as beef and poultry.

SOUTH LOUISIANA POTATO SALAD

BOILED POTATOES

5 cups water
3 teaspoons liquid crab boil

4 pounds red new potatoes, skins on

In a medium pot, combine water and crab boil. Bring to a boil. Add potatoes. Cook over high heat until potatoes are tender. Drain and set aside.

POTATO SALAD

Boiled potatoes
¼ cup finely chopped yellow onions
¼ cup finely chopped green bell peppers
¼ cup finely chopped celery
1 cup mayonnaise
¼ cup dill relish
¼ cup sweet relish

2 tablespoons Dijon-style mustard
1½ teaspoons granulated garlic
1 tablespoon plus 1 teaspoon salt
5 boiled eggs, diced
¼ cup chopped green onions

Chop potatoes that were set aside. In a large bowl, combine chopped potatoes and all remaining ingredients. Mix well. Refrigerate and serve.

Serves 6 to 8 people

If you don't have crab boil, just add ½ teaspoon of cayenne pepper. If you like it hot like I do, you can use both. Great with fried foods! You can use whatever type of potato you like. I find red new potatoes are best in this recipe.

MIKE ANDERSON'S

COLLEGE TOWN SEAFOOD

DESSERTS

Desserts

BREAD PUDDING

PUDDING

10 eggs
1   cup sugar
½   cup chopped pecans
1   cup sweetened
    condensed milk
2   tablespoons vanilla
    extract
4   (12-ounce) cans
    evaporated milk

1   cup raisins, soaked in
    warm water and
    drained
Vegetable spray
4   tablespoons ground
    cinnamon, divided
1   loaf French bread,
    sliced
Rum sauce

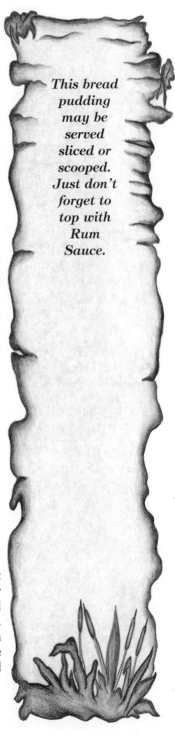

This bread pudding may be served sliced or scooped. Just don't forget to top with Rum Sauce.

Combine eggs, sugar, pecans, condensed milk, vanilla extract, evaporated milk and raisins. Stir well. Line a 9-inch springform pan with 3-inch sides with aluminum foil. Spray foil with vegetable spray. Sprinkle 2 tablespoons of cinnamon in bottom of pan. Put bread in pan. Pour mixture over bread. Allow bread to absorb mixture. Top with remaining 2 tablespoons cinnamon. Cover with aluminum foil. Bake 1½ hours at 350°. Uncover and cook 15 to 20 minutes until brown. Slice. Top with our Rum Sauce. Serve hot.

Serves 10 to 12 people

RUM SAUCE

1   cup half-and-half
2   sticks butter or
    margarine
1   cup brown sugar

2   teaspoons ground
    cinnamon
¾   cup light rum

In a small saucepan, warm half-and-half over low heat. Set aside. In a separate small pot, melt butter. Add brown sugar and cinnamon. Using a wire whisk, stir mixture until thickened. Bring mixture to a boil being careful not to burn. Add rum. Stir. Using long matches, light mixture. Let rum sauce burn a few seconds. Pour half-and-half over mixture to extinguish flames. Stir. Warm over low heat until thickened. Serve over bread pudding.

Yield: 2 cups

LOUISIANA SNOWBALL

I suggest wearing plastic gloves while making the Louisiana Snowball. I sometimes roll the ice cream in other kinds of nuts or candies. Use your imagination. If you have children, let them help with this dessert. I am sure they will create a new meaning for "finger-lickin' good."

¾ cup vanilla ice cream
⅓ cup chopped toasted
    pecans

¼ cup toasted coconut
    flakes

Mold ice cream into a ball. Roll ice cream ball into pecans and coconut. Put into a plastic bag or wrap with plastic wrap. Freeze 6 to 8 hours. Before serving, top with rum sauce, chocolate syrup, or both.

Serves 1 person

SWAMP PIE

CRUST

1 stick margarine, melted	3 cups graham cracker crumbs

Mix margarine and graham cracker crumbs. Lightly pat into a 9-inch springform pan with 3-inch sides. Bake 10 minutes at 350°. Let cool.

FILLING

¾ cup chocolate syrup	1 cup toasted almonds
½ gallon vanilla ice cream	1 cup toasted coconut
	¾ cup whipped cream

BOTTOM LAYER:

Pour ¼ cup chocolate syrup on bottom. Add a layer of ice cream. Firmly pack. Swirl another ¼ cup of chocolate syrup over ice cream. Sprinkle ⅓ cup toasted almonds and ⅓ cup of toasted coconut on top chocolate syrup.

MIDDLE LAYER:

Add another layer of ice cream. Firmly pack. Swirl ¼ cup chocolate syrup on ice cream. Sprinkle ⅓ cup of toasted almonds and ⅓ cup of toasted coconut on top of chocolate syrup.

TOP LAYER:

Spread ¾ cup whip cream over middle layer. Sprinkle remaining almonds and coconut on top. Freeze.

Serves 8 people

After pie is made, slice before freezing. This recipe may seem difficult at first glance, but quite the opposite, just a little time consuming.

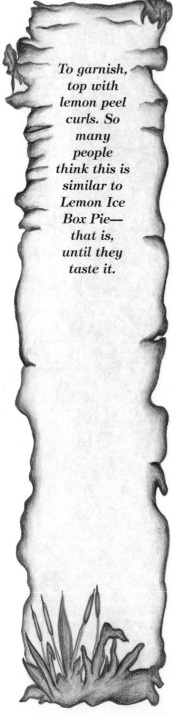

LEMONADE PIE

To garnish, top with lemon peel curls. So many people think this is similar to Lemon Ice Box Pie— that is, until they taste it.

CRUST

1	stick margarine, melted	1½	cups graham cracker crumbs

Mix ingredients together and lightly pat into a standard pie pan. Bake in oven for 10 minutes at 350°. Cool before adding filling.

FILLING

½	cup fresh lemon juice	1	(14-ounce) can sweetened condensed milk
1	lemon with peel, finely chopped		
⅓	cup sugar	2	cups whipped cream

Add lemon juice, chopped lemon and sugar to a blender. Blend well. Strain blended mixture into a mixing bowl. Add condensed milk. Using a mixer, whip well. Fold whipped cream into mixture. Pour into crust. Smooth top with a spatula. Cut and freeze.

Serves 8 people

CHEESECAKE

CRUST

1	stick margarine, melted	3	cups graham cracker crumbs

Mix ingredients well. Lightly pat into a 9-inch springform pan with 3-inch sides. Bake in oven for 10 minutes on 350°. Let cool.

FILLING

2½	pounds cream cheese, softened	1	tablespoon vanilla extract
	Juice of one lemon	8	eggs
1	cup sugar	2	egg yolks
1	tablespoon self-rising flour	1	cup half-and-half

Combine all filling ingredients in a mixing bowl. Using an electric mixer, whip until smooth. Pour whipped mixture into crust. Cover with aluminum foil. Bake 3½ hours at 300°. Take cheesecake out and set aside for 1 hour. Uncover cheesecake. Bake at 350° another 15 minutes or until brown. Let cool. Refrigerate until ready to serve.

Serves 10 to 12 people

I like my cheesecake plain and then topped with fruit or a sauce of some kind. In the restaurant, we serve the cheesecake topped with Amaretto, fresh strawberries or chocolate sauce.

Sweet Potato Pecan Pie

3	medium sweet potatoes	¼	teaspoon salt
¾	cup sugar, divided	½	teaspoon vanilla extract
¾	cup low-fat milk	2	tablespoons butter or
1	tablespoon ground cinnamon		margarine, melted
1	tablespoon self-rising flour	1	teaspoon all-purpose flour
2	eggs	12	(4-inch) pie shells
¾	cup light corn syrup	4	cups chopped pecans

Bake sweet potatoes 30 minutes at 350°. Peel and place in medium bowl. Add ¼ cup sugar, milk, cinnamon and self-rising flour. Stir well. Set aside. In a separate bowl, add eggs, corn syrup, salt, vanilla extract, butter, all-purpose flour and remaining ½ cup sugar. Stir well. Place pie shells on a baking sheet. Add ¼ cup of sweet potato mixture to each pie shell. Top each with ¼ cup of syrup mixture. Sprinkle chopped pecans on top of pies. Bake 25 to 30 minutes at 375°. Let stand 15 to 20 minutes before serving. Serve hot or cold.

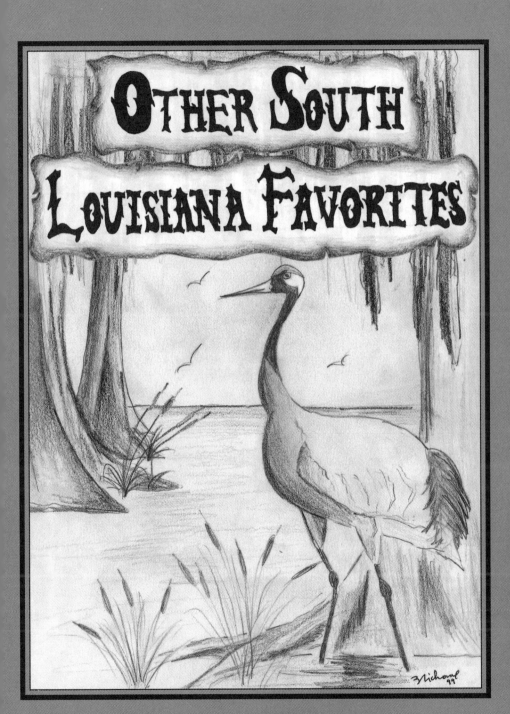

Other South Louisiana Favorites

Other South Louisiana Favorites

BLUEBERRY CRUNCH

1 cup all-purpose flour	½ cup granulated sugar
1½ sticks butter	1 (21-ounce) can
½ cup chopped pecans	blueberry pie filling
1 (8-ounce) package	1 (8-ounce) carton Cool
cream cheese, room	Whip, thawed
temperature	

In a large bowl, combine flour and butter. Mix well. Add chopped pecans. Spread into a greased 9x13-inch baking pan. Bake 15 minutes at 350°. Set aside to cool. In a separate mixing bowl, combine cream cheese and sugar. Blend well. Spread mixture on top of crust. Spread blueberry pie filling on top of cream cheese mixture. Top with Cool Whip.

Mary F. Anderson (Mike Anderson's mother)

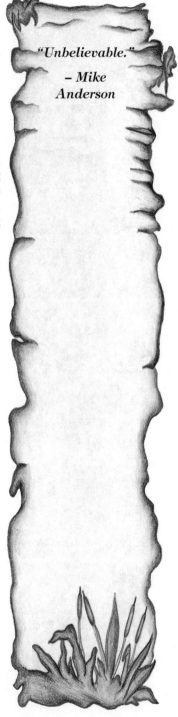

"Unbelievable."

– Mike Anderson

CUCUMBER RED HOT PICKLES

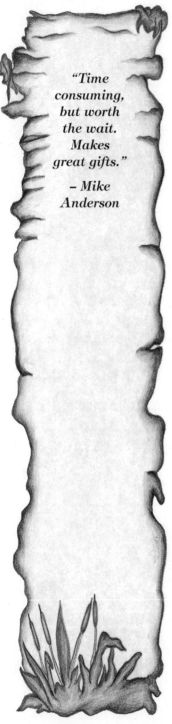

"Time consuming, but worth the wait. Makes great gifts."

– Mike Anderson

STEP 1

7	large cucumbers	1	gallon water
1	cup pickling lime	1	gallon ice water

Peel and core cucumbers. Slice into rings. Soak cucumber rings 24 hours in pickling lime and water. Drain. Soak in ice water 3 hours. Drain.

STEP 2

1	cup white vinegar	1	bottle red food
1	tablespoon alum		coloring
		Water	

In a large pot, combine vinegar, alum and food coloring. Add drained cucumbers from Step 1. Add enough water to pot to cover cucumbers. Cover and simmer 2 hours. Drain. Place cucumbers in a large bowl.

STEP 3

2	cups water	1	large package
2	cups white vinegar		cinnamon red hots
10	cups granulated sugar		candy
8	cinnamon sticks		

Combine all ingredients in a large pot. Bring mixture to a boil. Pour boiling mixture over cucumbers. Soak 24 hours.

STEP 4

Drain cucumbers, reserving drained liquid. In a large pot bring reserved liquid back to a boil. Pour over cucumbers again. Soak 24 hours.

STEP 5

Drain cucumbers, reserving drained liquid. Put drained cucumbers into jars. In a large pot bring reserved liquid back to a boil. Pour over cucumbers. Close and seal jars.

Mary F. Anderson (Mike Anderson's mother)

MARY F. ANDERSON'S SQUASH CASSEROLE

8	medium yellow summer squash
½	cup mayonnaise
2	tablespoons grated yellow onions
⅔	cup grated sharp cheddar cheese
½	cup milk
	Salt and pepper
	Cracker crumbs
	Butter

Cook squash, drain and mash. In a large bowl, mix squash, mayonnaise, grated onions, grated cheese and milk. Mix well. Salt and pepper to taste. Pour into a greased baking dish. Bake at 400° until lightly brown. Crumble crackers onto a cookie sheet. Bake in butter until toasted. Sprinkle cracker crumbs on top of squash casserole. Cook another 5 minutes. Serve hot.

Mary F. Anderson (Mike Anderson's mother)

"The Best."
– Mike Anderson

PEAR RELISH

6-8	pounds pears, chopped
4	large yellow onions, chopped
4	red bell peppers, chopped
4	green bell peppers, chopped
4	cups white vinegar
4	cups granulated sugar
2	tablespoons celery seed
1	teaspoon mustard seed
1	teaspoon salt
1	tablespoon mixed pickling spice
	Cayenne pepper

Combine pears, onions and red and green bell peppers in a food processor. Process until finely chopped. Drain. In a large pot, add processed mixture, vinegar, sugar, celery seed, mustard seed, salt and mixed pickling spice. Add desired amount of cayenne pepper. Bring to a low boil. Let boil for 1 hour or until thick. Fill jars and seal.

"Try this on peas or butter beans."
– Mike Anderson

Mary F. Anderson (Mike Anderson's mother)

145

Mike Anderson

MARY F. ANDERSON'S SALAD DRESSING

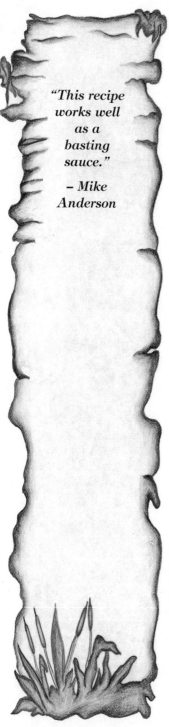

"This recipe works well as a basting sauce."

– Mike Anderson

2 tablespoons salt
1 teaspoon black pepper
1 teaspoon hot sauce
1 teaspoon paprika
1 tablespoon Worcestershire sauce
2 tablespoons mustard

2 tablespoons finely chopped yellow onions
1 teaspoon finely chopped garlic
1 cup vegetable oil
1 cup white vinegar
1 tablespoon lemon juice

In a large bowl, combine salt, pepper, hot sauce, paprika, Worcestershire sauce, mustard, chopped onions and garlic. Mix well while crushing onions and garlic. Add oil. Stir. Add vinegar and lemon juice. Stir. Chill before serving.

Mary F. Anderson (Mike Anderson's mother)

ANGEL FOOD DELIGHT

1 large angel food cake, torn into pieces
1 (14-ounce) can fat-free condensed milk
2 cups fresh berries

1 cup canned berries, drained
1 (8-ounce) carton frozen whipped topping, thawed

Break angel food cake into bite-sized pieces. Place ¼ cake pieces in bottom of serving bowl. Drizzle 3 ounces condensed milk over cake. Add ½ cup of fresh berries and ¼ cup canned berries. Spread a layer of whipped topping. Repeat these steps 3 more times. Garnish with fresh berries on top.

Summer Anderson

DIVINITY

4	cups granulated sugar	1	teaspoon vanilla
½	cup water		extract
1	cup light corn syrup	1	cup chopped pecans
3	egg whites, stiffly		(optional)
	beaten		Vegetable spray

In a large saucepan, combine sugar, water and corn syrup. Cook over low heat until soft ball is formed. In a separate bowl, pour ⅓ of mixture over stiffly beaten egg whites. Stir constantly. Set aside. Cook remaining mixture to a firm ball. Add to egg white mixture. Stir constantly. Add vanilla. Stir until mixture starts to thicken. Add nuts if desired. Spray a sheet of waxed paper with vegetable spray. Drop by spoonfuls onto waxed paper. Let harden.

Summer Anderson

"This was one of Granny and Mina's favorites at Christmastime at my home. They just loved those 'pulverized' pecans."

– Summer

HOT CINNAMON CANDY

4	cups granulated sugar	2-3	teaspoons cinnamon
1¾	cups light corn syrup		oil
1	cup water	1	teaspoon red or green
			food coloring

Lightly grease a 10x15-inch baking pan. Set aside. In a large saucepan, combine sugar, corn syrup and water. Boil over moderate heat. Tap bottom of pan with a wooden spoon to help dissolve sugar. If candy thermometer is available, place in pan. Without stirring, continue to boil until mixture reaches the "hard cracked" stage (300°). This can be determined by spooning a small amount of mixture into cold water. If it forms hard brittle threads, quickly remove pan from heat. Add cinnamon oil and food coloring. Stir well. Pour mixture into prepared baking pan. When candy has cooled and hardened, break using a mallet or rolling pin. Store in airtight containers.

Yield: 2¼ pounds

Michael Anderson II and Summer Anderson

"This recipe is almost as old as we are."

– Summer and Michael

MARY'S INFAMOUS CRAWFISH SOUP

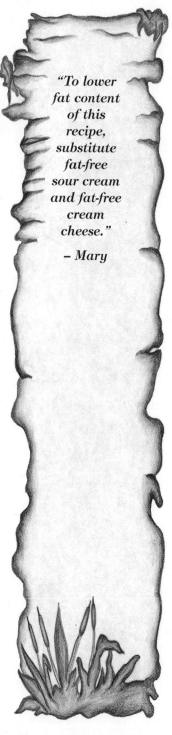

"To lower fat content of this recipe, substitute fat-free sour cream and fat-free cream cheese."

– Mary

4	cups chopped yellow onions	2	(8-ounce) packages cream cheese
2	sticks butter or margarine	2	cups sour cream
4	cups heavy cream		Salt and pepper
1	teaspoon cayenne pepper	2-3	pounds crawfish tails
		1	cup chopped green onions

In a large pot, sauté yellow onions in butter or margarine. Add heavy cream, cayenne pepper, cream cheese and sour cream. Add salt and pepper to taste. Mix well. Simmer 1 hour. Add crawfish tails. Simmer over low heat 30 minutes. Add green onions before serving.

Serves 6 to 8 people

Mary M. Anderson

148

MICHAEL'S "DYNAMITE" PORK TENDERLOIN

MARINADE

1 cup soy sauce	2 tablespoons Mike Anderson's South Louisiana Seasoning or Season All
¼ cup honey	

Combine all ingredients. Mix well.

TENDERLOIN

2 pound boneless pork tenderloin	¼ cup sliced jalapeño peppers
1 (8-ounce) package cream cheese, room temperature	

Marinate tenderloin 2 to 4 hours. Cut tenderloin lengthwise down center and fill with cream cheese. Top with jalapeño peppers and fold tenderloin back together. Place tenderloin on "hot" coals 10 to 20 minutes.

Michael H. Anderson II

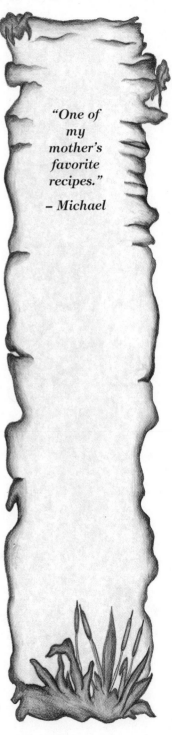

"One of my mother's favorite recipes."

– Michael

Quick and Easy Bananas Foster

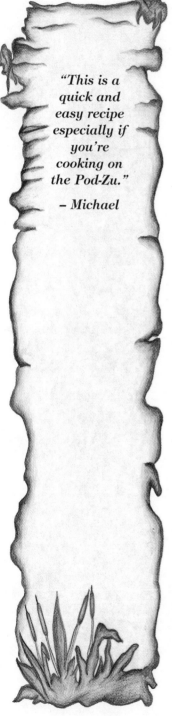

"This is a quick and easy recipe especially if you're cooking on the Pod-Zu."

– Michael

6	tablespoons butter	4	bananas, sliced
⅓	cup brown sugar		lengthwise
1	teaspoon ground	½	cup dark rum
	cinnamon		Vanilla ice cream
1	teaspoon vanilla		
	extract		

In a small saucepan, melt butter. Add brown sugar and cinnamon. Stir. Add vanilla extract, sliced bananas and rum. Stir well. Using matches, light rum. Let rum burn off. Stir. Serve over vanilla ice cream

Serves 4 to 6 people

Michael H. Anderson II

Rice Dressing

1	pound ground chuck	4	cups chopped green
1	pound lean ground		onions
	pork sausage	6	cups cooked rice
½	cup chicken livers	2	tablespoons chopped
3	cups chopped yellow		parsley
	onions		

In a large saucepan, brown ground chuck and ground pork sausage. Using a food processor, chop chicken livers. Add chopped livers, yellow onions and green onions to saucepan. Cook 30 minutes. Add rice. Mix well. Pour mixture into a casserole dish. Bake 30 minutes at 375°. Sprinkle parsley on top and serve.

Mary M. Anderson

SUMMER'S SENSATIONAL SALAD

SALAD DRESSING

1   package Italian salad
    dressing mix (olive
    oil and balsamic
    vinegar)

1   tablespoon anchovy
    paste
4   cloves fresh garlic,
    minced

Combine all ingredients. Stir. Refrigerate until ready to serve.

CROUTONS

1   tablespoon olive oil
1   teaspoon Mike
    Anderson's South
    Louisiana Seasoning
    or Season All

4   slices bread, cubed

In a small bowl, combine olive oil and Mike Anderson's South Louisiana Seasoning or Season All. Stir well. Place cubes of bread on cookie sheet. Pour contents of bowl over bread. Bake at 350° until golden brown. Let cool.

SALAD

1   head romaine lettuce
Salad Dressing
Feta cheese
Fresh ground black pepper

Fresh grated Romano
    and Parmesan cheese
Croutons

Tear lettuce into a bowl. Add dressing and toss. Sprinkle feta cheese on top of salad. Grind black pepper. Sprinkle Romano and Parmesan cheese over top. Top with croutons and serve.

Summer Anderson

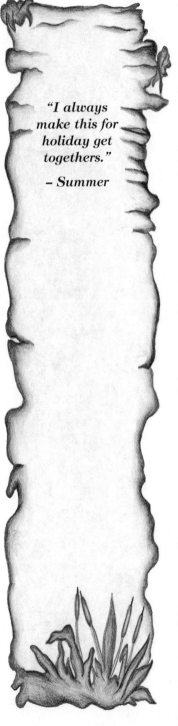

"I always make this for holiday get togethers."

– Summer

ADELE'S ITALIAN CHICKEN

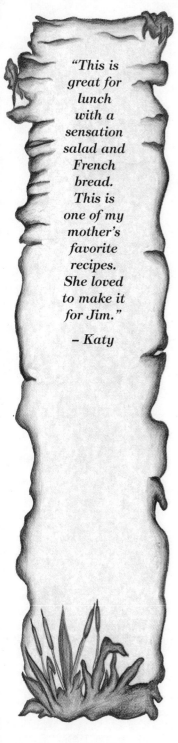

"This is great for lunch with a sensation salad and French bread. This is one of my mother's favorite recipes. She loved to make it for Jim."

– Katy

1½	cups Italian bread crumbs	4	tablespoons butter or margarine, melted
½	cup Parmesan cheese		Vegetable spray
8-10	boneless chicken strips		

In a medium bowl, combine bread crumbs and Parmesan cheese. Stir. Dip each chicken strip in melted butter or margarine, then roll in bread crumb and cheese mixture. Repeat this step for each chicken strip. Coat a large baking sheet with vegetable spray. Place the chicken strips on baking sheet. Bake 30 minutes at 350°.

Katy and Jim Adams

OYSTER DE BARK

4	tablespoons butter or margarine	1	dozen oysters on the half shell
6	tablespoons extra virgin olive oil	3	tablespoons chopped parsley
2-3	tablespoons fresh minced garlic	1	tablespoon paprika
½	cup white wine	3	tablespoons fresh grated Parmesan cheese
Juice of ½ a lemon			
1	teaspoon black pepper		

In a small saucepan, combine butter or margarine and olive oil. Bring to a simmer. Add garlic. Sauté over low heat 10 to 15 minutes (being careful not to burn). Add white wine, lemon juice and black pepper. Simmer over low heat 5 minutes. Set aside. Place oysters in shell on grill or BBQ pit. Spoon wine sauce on top of oysters until shell is full. Cook over medium heat until liquid inside oyster shells begins to simmer. Sprinkle parsley, paprika and Parmesan cheese on top of oysters. Cook until oysters shrink. Serve in oyster shell.

Dennis Barkemeyer Jr.

"Slice French bread and spread leftover sauce on one side. Place bread on grill, sauce side down, for two minutes. This makes a good garlic bread. My dad taught me this recipe."

– Dennis

NOTHIN' LIKE SPINACH

"Great side dish with seafood or meat dishes. Easy-quick-delicious! We hope this dish tastes as good in Baton Rouge as it does in Hattiesburg."

– Brad and Peggy

2 packages frozen chopped spinach	1 (8-ounce) package cream cheese
1 (10¾-ounce) can condensed cream of mushroom soup	1 (2.8-ounce) can onion rings

Cook spinach according to directions on package. Drain well and set aside. In a separate bowl, combine mushroom soup and cream cheese. Mix well. Add spinach. Mix. Pour into an ungreased 1½-quart baking dish. Cook, uncovered, 20 minutes at 375°. Sprinkle onion rings on top. Bake another 15 minutes.

Brad and Peggy Brian

ABBEVILLE CHOW CHOW

2	large mirlitons	9	cups white vinegar, divided
3	large cucumbers	6	cups water
4-5	stalks celery	1	cup flour
7	large yellow onions	3	cups granulated sugar
1	large head cauliflower	½	box turmeric
2	pounds artichokes, ground	3	(1-ounce) boxes dried mustard
2	(4-ounce) cans diced pimento	2	cups vegetable oil
Salt			

Clean mirlitons, cucumbers, celery, onions and cauliflower thoroughly and chop into small pieces (not too small). In a large bowl combine chopped vegetables, artichokes and pimento. Season well with salt. Let stand 1 hour, stirring now and then to make sure salt is evenly distributed. Drain mixture well using a colander. Set aside. In a medium pot, briskly boil 6 cups vinegar and 6 cups water. Pour over vegetables, scalding them. Let stand 30 minutes. Drain well. Using a cheese cloth bag, drain over night. Set aside. In a separate pot, boil 2 cups vinegar. In a large bowl, combine boiled vinegar, flour, sugar, turmeric, dry mustard, remaining 1 cup cold vinegar and vegetable oil. Stir constantly until thickened. Add well-drained vegetables. Cook over low heat, 20 to 30 minutes. Remove from stove. Pour into jars or airtight containers.

Yield: 2 pints

Dr. Marty Broussard

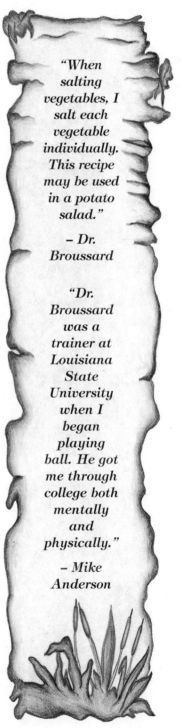

"When salting vegetables, I salt each vegetable individually. This recipe may be used in a potato salad."

– Dr. Broussard

"Dr. Broussard was a trainer at Louisiana State University when I began playing ball. He got me through college both mentally and physically."

– Mike Anderson

JAN'S MEATLOAF

"Sweet 'n Low can be substituted for brown sugar if dieting, but brown sugar is much better. This also can be made ahead of time separately and used when needed."

– Jan

SAUCE

2	(8-ounce) cans tomato sauce	4	heaping tablespoons brown sugar
4-5	tablespoons Worcestershire sauce	¼	teaspoon salt
		¼	teaspoon black pepper

Mix all ingredients well. Refrigerate until ready to use.

MEAT

	Vegetable spray	5	tablespoons butter or margarine
1	large yellow onion, chopped	3	pounds lean ground chuck
1	large bell pepper, chopped		Salt and pepper
			Granulated garlic

Spray vegetable spray in a large square baking dish. Set aside. In a small saucepan, sauté onions and bell peppers in butter or margarine until tender. In a large bowl, combine sautéed vegetables and lean ground chuck. Season to taste with salt, pepper and granulated garlic. Mix well. Spread in baking dish. Bake 45 minutes at 375° or until meat is almost done. Cut meat into squares, leaving them in dish. Pour sauce on top of meat, allowing it to go down between squares. Bake another 20 minutes at 375°. Serve over mashed potatoes.

Jan Brown

CONGEALED SALAD

1 (8-ounce) can crushed
  pineapple (do not
  drain)
1 (11-ounce) can
  Mandarin oranges
  (do not drain)

2 (3-ounce) packages
  apricot-flavored
  gelatin
2 cups buttermilk
1 (8-ounce) container
  Cool Whip

Pour undrained pineapples and Mandarin oranges into a
saucepan and heat. Dissolve gelatin in heated juices. Cool
30 minutes. Add buttermilk and Cool Whip. Pour into a
mold. Refrigerate until firm.

Marilyn M. Contois

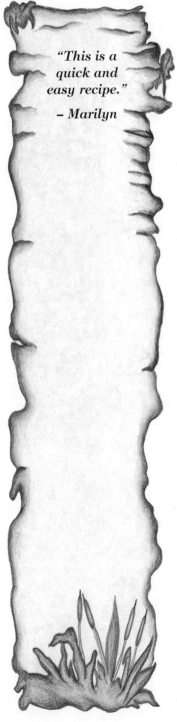

*"This is a
quick and
easy recipe."*

– Marilyn

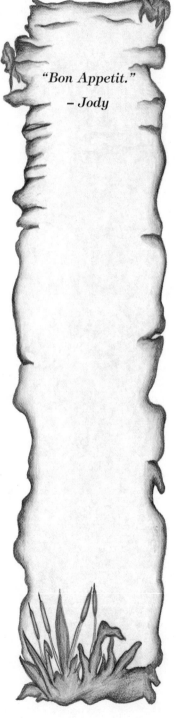

JODY'S CRAWFISH OR SHRIMP FETTUCCINI CASSEROLE

"Bon Appetit."

– Jody

1 large yellow onion, chopped
1 green bell pepper, chopped
1 celery stalk, chopped
1 stick butter
½ cup all-purpose flour
½ cup cream sherry or ½ cup water
1 pound crawfish tails or fresh, peeled shrimp
1¼ tablespoons parsley flakes

1 cup half-and-half or heavy cream
⅓ pound Velveeta jalapeño cheese, cubed
1 tablespoon fresh garlic, crushed
Salt and pepper
¾-1 pound frozen fettuccini noodles, cooked and drained
Grated Parmesan cheese

Using a heavy saucepan, sauté onions, bell peppers and celery in butter. Cook 10 minutes or until tender. Add flour. Stir well. Cook 10 minutes over low heat. Stir constantly. Add sherry or water and cook another 5 minutes. Add crawfish or shrimp and parsley. Cook 10 minutes. Stir frequently. Add half-and-half or cream, Velveeta cheese and garlic. Mix well. Add salt and pepper to taste. Cook 5 minutes over low heat. Stir frequently. Fold fettuccini noodles into crawfish/shrimp sauce. Mix gently. Pour into 2 quart, greased casserole dish. Sprinkle Parmesan cheese on top, covering thoroughly. Bake 30 minutes at 350°.

Serves 4 people

Jody Doucet

BREAKFAST CASSEROLE

10 slices white bread, divided
1 pound sausage or bacon
2 cups sharp cheddar cheese, shredded
2 cups mild cheddar cheese, shredded
¾ teaspoon dry mustard
3 cups milk
6 eggs
½ teaspoon salt
¼ teaspoon white pepper

Remove crusts from bread and cut into quarters. Set aside. Fry sausage or bacon and slice or crumble. Arrange half of bread squares in a lightly greased 9x13-inch baking pan. Top with a layer of sharp cheese, cooked meat, bread squares and mild cheese. In a separate bowl, dissolve mustard in milk. Add eggs, salt and pepper to bowl. Beat mixture. Pour mixture over layers, cover and refrigerate overnight. Bake, uncovered, 1 hour at 350° or until firm and brown.

Kathy Emory

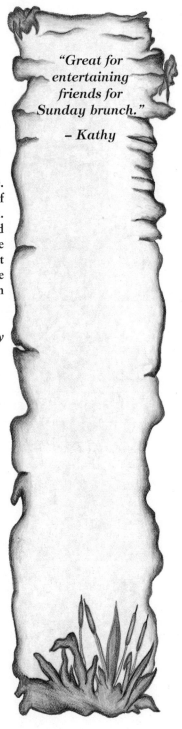

"Great for entertaining friends for Sunday brunch."

– Kathy

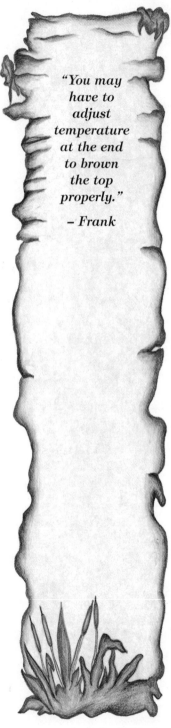

*"You may
have to
adjust
temperature
at the end
to brown
the top
properly."*

– Frank

ARTICHOKE LASAGNA

BÉCHAMEL SAUCE

2	cups milk	3	tablespoons flour
4	tablespoons butter	¼	teaspoon salt

In a small saucepan, combine all ingredients. Simmer over low heat until butter is melted. Remove from heat and set aside.

LASAGNA

Homemade lasagna
   noodles
4-5 medium artichokes,
   cooked, scraped and
   chopped

Béchamel sauce
1 stick butter
⅔ cup grated Parmesan
   cheese

Cook homemade lasagna noodles and rinse with cold water. Scrape off excess moisture. Line a greased lasagna pan with a layer of noodles. Combine artichokes and Béchamel sauce. Spread a light and even layer of mixture over noodles. Dot with butter. Sprinkle with Parmesan cheese. Repeat layers 6 times. Top with noodles and a thin layer of Béchamel sauce. Dot with butter and sprinkle Parmesan cheese on top. Bake 10 minutes at 400° or until a golden crust has formed. Let rest for 10 minutes before serving

Frank Grumpert III

COACH HAMLEY'S "FRE-OLIES"

1	pound dry pinto beans, soaked, drained and rinsed
2	large yellow onions, chopped
1	(10-ounce) can Rotel tomatoes

	Salt to taste
1	pound ground chuck
1	pound smoked sausage
1	large bag small corn chips

In a medium pot, combine beans, onions, tomatoes and salt. Add enough water to completely cover beans and vegetables. Stir. Simmer 30 minutes over low to medium heat. Add ground chuck and sliced sausage. Simmer over low to medium heat, stirring frequently until beans are done. Spoon over corn chips and serve.

Serves 6 to 8 people

Ann Hamley

"When Coach Hamley first came to LSU, he was a widower. He had to come up with a recipe that was quick and easy for entertaining his post game guests. This was perfect."

– Ann

LE BONE'S BBQ SHRIMP

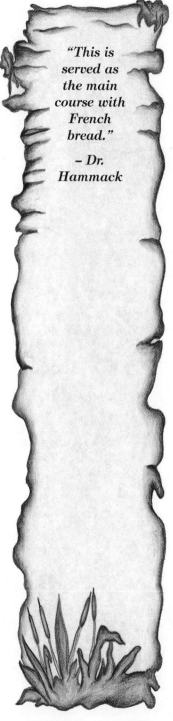

"This is served as the main course with French bread."

– Dr. Hammack

2 tablespoons olive oil	Fresh minced garlic
2 sticks butter, divided	Cayenne pepper
2-4 pounds fresh, peeled 15 to 20 count shrimp	Juice of 1 lemon
	Hot sauce
Italian seasoning	1 large purple onion, slice into rings
Lemon pepper	1-2 lemons, sliced
Black pepper	

Using a rectangular cake pan, spread olive oil on bottom of pan. Cut 1 stick of butter into squares and spread on bottom of the pan. Place shrimp on top of butter pats as a third layer. Sprinkle Italian seasoning and lemon pepper generously on top of shrimp. Sprinkle black pepper and minced garlic to taste on top of shrimp. Lightly sprinkle cayenne pepper. Pour lemon juice on top of shrimp. Cut remaining stick of butter into squares and spread over shrimp and seasonings. Add desired amount of hot sauce, onion slices and lemon slices. Cover with tin foil and bake 30 minutes at 350°

Dr. Jimmie Hammack

162

CHICKEN CHALUPAS

2	(10¾-ounce) cans condensed cream of chicken soup	¾	pound shredded Monterey Jack cheese, divided
1	(4-ounce) can chopped green chiles	¾	pound shredded Longhorn cheese, divided
1	small yellow onion, chopped	4	raw boneless, skinless chicken breast, cubed
¾	cup chopped green onions	12	medium flour tortillas
1	pint sour cream	Paprika	
1	cup sliced black olives		

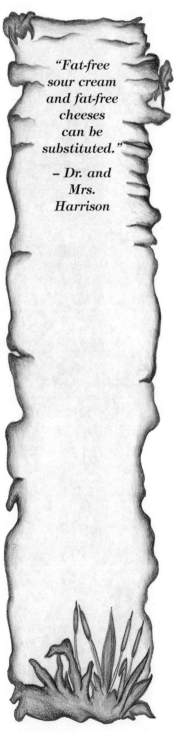

"Fat-free sour cream and fat-free cheeses can be substituted."

– Dr. and Mrs. Harrison

In a large bowl, combine soup, green chiles, yellow onions, green onions, sour cream and black olives. Add ½ pound of Monterey Jack cheese and ½ pound of Longhorn cheese. Mix well. Set aside 2 cups of mixture. Add cubed chicken to large bowl. Stir. Spoon 2 to 4 tablespoons of chicken mixture onto each flour tortilla and tri-fold. Place each folded tortilla in a greased 9x13-inch casserole dish, seam side down. Spread 2 cups of mixture previously set aside over tortillas. Sprinkle remaining cheeses on top. Sprinkle paprika on top of cheese. Cover casserole dish with aluminum foil and bake 35 minutes at 350°. Remove foil and bake 5 to 10 minutes longer.

Serves 6 to 8 people

Dr. and Mrs. George Harrison

LIGHTHORSE'S "CHICKEN NECK" STOCK

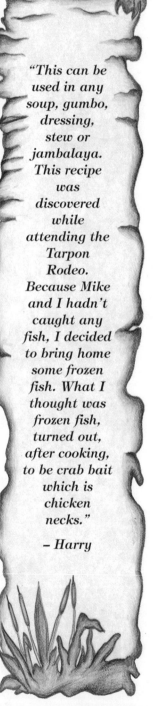

"This can be used in any soup, gumbo, dressing, stew or jambalaya. This recipe was discovered while attending the Tarpon Rodeo. Because Mike and I hadn't caught any fish, I decided to bring home some frozen fish. What I thought was frozen fish, turned out, after cooking, to be crab bait which is chicken necks."

– Harry

16	cups water	1	teaspoon of hot sauce (to add a little kick!)
1	tablespoon lemon pepper	1	clove garlic, chopped
1	tablespoon Mike Anderson's South Louisiana Seasoning or Season All	2-3	large yellow onions, chopped
		2	green bell peppers, chopped
2	tablespoons Italian seasoning	4-5	stalks celery, chopped
½	bunch parsley stems, chopped	2	pounds chicken necks

In a large pot, combine all ingredients except chicken necks. Bring mixture to a boil. Let boil approximately 30 minutes to 1 hour. Add chicken necks. Reduce heat and cook 1 hour longer. Strain mixture. Remove meat from bones for a later use. Freeze.

Harry "Lighthorse" Heroman Jr.

SHRIMP OVER ANGEL HAIR

1	yellow onion chopped	2	cups fresh, peeled shrimp
4	cloves garlic, chopped		
1	stick butter	½	teaspoon salt
½	teaspoon liquid crab boil	½	teaspoon black pepper
½	cup white wine	1	(12-ounce) package angel hair pasta, cooked and drained
¼	cup fresh chopped parsley	¾	cup freshly grated Parmesan cheese

In a medium saucepan, sauté onions and garlic in butter. Simmer over low heat until onions are translucent. Stir frequently. Add liquid crab boil, white wine and parsley. Stir. Add shrimp, salt and pepper. Cook until shrimp are done. Pour over cooked angel hair pasta. Top with Parmesan cheese and serve.

Serves 6 to 8 people

Tommy Hodson

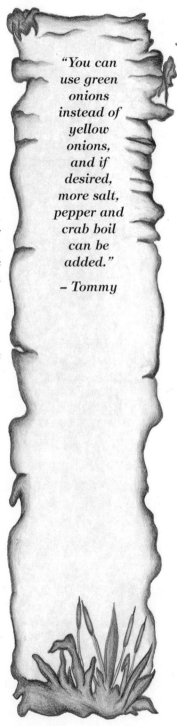

"You can use green onions instead of yellow onions, and if desired, more salt, pepper and crab boil can be added."

– Tommy

MINA'S PECAN PRALINES

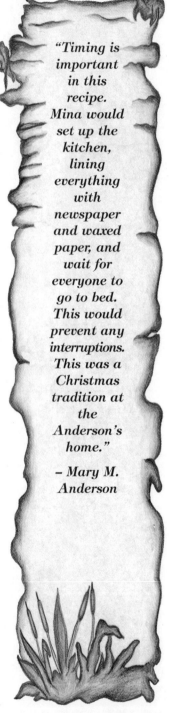

"Timing is important in this recipe. Mina would set up the kitchen, lining everything with newspaper and waxed paper, and wait for everyone to go to bed. This would prevent any interruptions. This was a Christmas tradition at the Anderson's home."

– Mary M. Anderson

2	cups granulated sugar	3	cups chopped pecans
1	cup brown sugar	1	teaspoon vanilla extract
1	tablespoon light corn syrup	½	teaspoon almond extract
1	stick butter		
1	cup evaporated milk		

Bring all ingredients to a boil and simmer 25 minutes or until candy forms a hard ball. Remove from heat. Cool 10 minutes. Spoon onto waxed paper.

Mina Jones

GARLIC CHEESE GRITS

1	cup grits	¼	teaspoon
2	teaspoons salt		Worcestershire sauce
4	cups water	1	garlic cheese roll,
1	teaspoon black pepper		cubed
4	tablespoons butter or	Paprika	
	margarine		

Cook grits in salt and water. When done, add black pepper, butter or margarine, Worcestershire sauce and cheese roll. Stir. After cheese has melted, pour into a 1½-quart casserole dish. Sprinkle paprika on top. Bake 30 minutes at 350°.

Shirley Juban

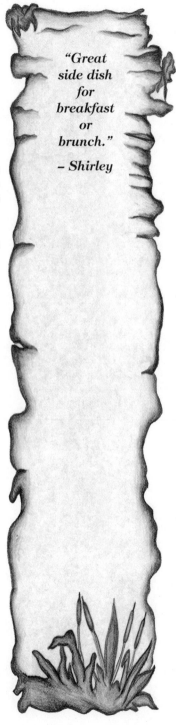

"Great side dish for breakfast or brunch."

– Shirley

GEORGE'S CHILI

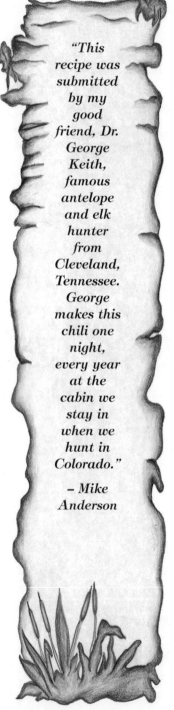

"This recipe was submitted by my good friend, Dr. George Keith, famous antelope and elk hunter from Cleveland, Tennessee. George makes this chili one night, every year at the cabin we stay in when we hunt in Colorado."

– Mike Anderson

1	pound ground round or wild game	1	(15-ounce) can diced tomatoes
1	pound steak, 1-inch cubes	Salt	
1	yellow onion, chopped	1	tablespoon cumin seeds
2	mild chile peppers or 1 large green bell pepper	1	tablespoon ground cumin
1	tablespoon black pepper	¼	cup chili powder
1	small can chipotle peppers	1	teaspoon cayenne pepper (optional)
1	(15-ounce) can tomato purée or sauce	¼	cup mesa flour
		¼	cup water
		1	can black beans (kidney or pinto beans)

Brown first five ingredients until pepper and onions are caramelized. Add chipotle peppers, tomato purée, diced tomatoes and salt to taste. Let simmer 15 minutes over low heat. Add cumin seeds, ground cumin, chili powder and cayenne pepper. Stir. Let simmer 1 hour. Add water if necessary. In a separate bowl, combine flour, water and beans. Add contents of bowl. Stir well. Let simmer until desired consistency.

Dr. George Keith

168

BASIC PIZZA

CRUST

1¼ cups warm water	1 tablespoon granulated
1 tablespoon yeast	sugar
½ teaspoon salt	¼ cup olive oil
½ teaspoon pepper	5 cups flour

In a large mixing bowl, combine water and yeast. Mix well. Add salt, pepper, sugar and oil. Using a whisk, whip well. Gradually add flour while constantly stirring. Using a wooden spoon, stir until mixture forms into a ball. On a floured surface, knead the dough until smooth. Place dough in a greased mixing bowl and cover. Let the dough rise until it has doubled in size. Punch down and divide into two equal balls. Spread each half in a greased pizza pan.

Yield: two (13½-inch) pizza crusts

SAUCE/TOPPING

4 cloves garlic, crushed	2 stalks fresh oregano
¼ cup olive oil	leaves, chopped
1 (15-ounce) can	1-2 cups shredded
tomato sauce	mozzarella cheese
4 fresh basil leaves,	Toppings of choice
chopped	

In a medium saucepan, sauté garlic in olive oil until golden brown. Add tomato sauce, basil and oregano. Simmer over low heat 20 minutes. Pour sauce on top of crust and spread to edges. Sprinkle mozzarella cheese on top of pizza and add desired toppings. Bake 20 to 30 minutes at 375°.

Lydia Kelly

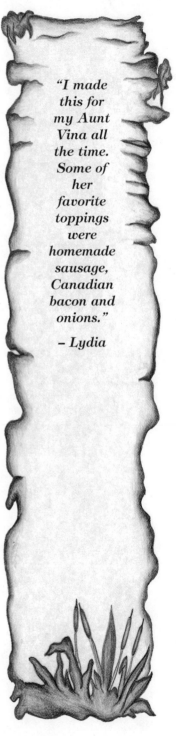

"I made this for my Aunt Vina all the time. Some of her favorite toppings were homemade sausage, Canadian bacon and onions."

– Lydia

POTATO SALAD

"When Granny and Nita got together, there could never be enough potato salad, cards and fun!"

– Mary M. Anderson

10-12 red potatoes
6   extra large eggs, boiled, peeled and diced
¼   cup finely chopped purple onions
¼   cup finely chopped celery
1   jar gherkins sweet pickles, drained and finely chopped
¼   teaspoon granulated sugar
1   cup mayonnaise
2   teaspoons mustard
¼   cup vegetable oil
Salt and pepper to taste

Cut potatoes into small cubes and cook in boiling water until tender. Drain well and set aside until cooled to room temperature. In a large bowl, combine all remaining ingredients. Mix well. When potatoes are cooled, fold in dressing mixture. Refrigerate and serve.

Nita Kessinger

WORLD'S BEST COOKIES

2	sticks butter	1	cup dry rolled oats
1	cup brown sugar	1¼	cups cornflakes
1	cup granulated sugar	1	cup coconut
2	eggs	¾	cup chopped pecans
1	cup vegetable oil	3½	cups sifted flour
2	teaspoons vanilla	1	teaspoon baking soda
	extract	1	teaspoon salt

Cream butter, brown sugar and granulated sugar until fluffy. Add eggs. Mix well. Add remaining ingredients in order. Mix well. Drop mixture by teaspoonfuls onto an ungreased baking sheet. Flatten with a fork dipped in water. Bake 12 minutes at 325° or until golden.

Nita Kessinger

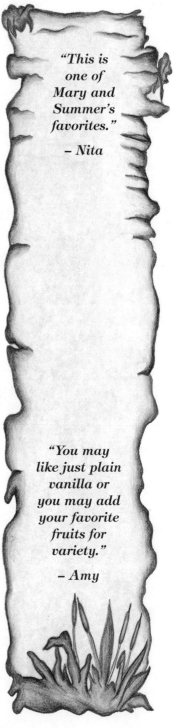

"This is one of Mary and Summer's favorites."

– Nita

AMY'S HOMEMADE ICE CREAM

2	teaspoons vanilla	3	(12-ounce) cans
	extract		evaporated milk
1	(14-ounce) can	4½	cups water
	sweetened	4	eggs, separated
	condensed milk	1¼	cups granulated sugar
			or more if desired

In a mixing bowl, combine vanilla, condensed milk, evaporated milk and water. Mix well. Cream egg yolks and sugar. Add to mixing bowl. Stir well. Beat egg whites until stiff and fold into mixture. Pour mixture into an electric freezer and wait until done.

Serves 10 to 12 people

Amy Lemoine

"You may like just plain vanilla or you may add your favorite fruits for variety."

– Amy

QUICK RUM CAKE

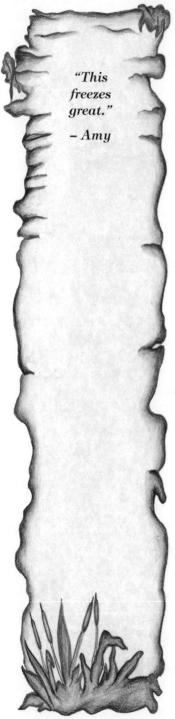

"This freezes great."

– Amy

CAKE

1	cup chopped pecans	1	(6-ounce) box French vanilla instant pudding
1	(18.25-ounce) box yellow cake mix (super, moist butter recipe, pudding in the mix)		
		½	cup water
		½	cup vegetable oil
		½	cup light rum
		4	eggs

Sprinkle chopped pecans in the bottom of a greased tube pan. In a separate bowl, combine cake mix, pudding mix, water, vegetable oil and rum. Stir well. Beat eggs and slowly add to bowl. Pour mixture into tube pan. Bake 1 hour at 325°. Cool in pan.

SAUCE

1	stick butter	¼	cup water
1	cup granulated sugar	¼	cup light rum

In a saucepan, combine all ingredients. Bring to a boil. Pour over baked cake while still in pan. Cool completely before removing cake from pan. The sauce will soak into the cake.

Amy Lemoine

LEAN SPINACH LASAGNA

¾ pound ground meat
½ yellow onion, chopped
½ teaspoon granulated
    garlic
1 teaspoon
    Worcestershire sauce
Salt and pepper
1 head broccoli
1 head cauliflower
1 cup baby carrots
2 packages frozen
    chopped spinach,
    drained
2 fresh squash, chopped
1 (8-ounce) can sliced
    mushrooms, drained

1 (16-ounce) jar
    spaghetti sauce
2 packages lasagna
    pasta, cooked and
    drained
1 (16-ounce) carton
    cottage cheese
1 package shredded
    mozzarella cheese
    (made with skim
    milk)
1 (3-ounce) package
    grated Parmesan
    cheese
1 (3-ounce) package
    grated Romano
    cheese

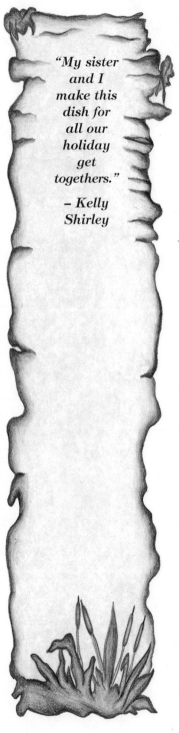

"My sister and I make this dish for all our holiday get togethers."

– Kelly Shirley

In a saucepan, combine ground meat, onions, garlic and Worcestershire sauce. Cook until meat is brown. Salt and pepper to taste. Drain and set aside. Steam broccoli, cauliflower, carrots, spinach and squash. Using a food processor, chop all steamed vegetables, mushrooms and previously set aside browned meat and onions. Pour chopped mixture into a mixing bowl. Add spaghetti sauce. Stir well. Layer ⅓ of lasagna noodles on bottom of baking dish. Next spread ⅓ of chopped mixture over noodles. Add a thin layer of cottage cheese. Sprinkle one-third package mozzarella cheese, 2 tablespoons grated Parmesan cheese and 2 tablespoons grated Romano cheese over cottage cheese. Repeat layers 2 more times. Bake 25 to 35 minutes at 275°.

Holly Shirley Little

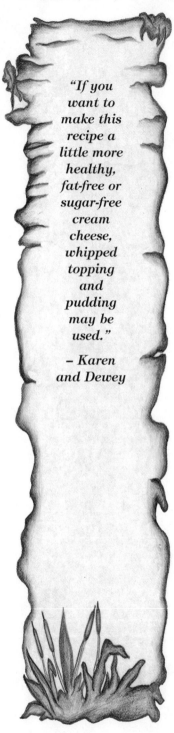

PISTACHIO DESSERT

CRUST

2	tablespoons granulated sugar	½	cup finely chopped pecans
1	cup all-purpose flour	1	stick margarine, melted

In a mixing bowl, combine sugar, flour, pecans and margarine. Mix well. Press into a greased 9x13-inch baking pan. Bake 15 minutes at 375°. Let cool.

FIRST LAYER

1	(8-ounce) package cream cheese, softened	⅔	cup powdered sugar
		¾	cup whipped topping

In a mixing bowl, combine cream cheese, powdered sugar and whipped topping. Mix well. Pour over crust.

SECOND LAYER

2	(3.4-ounce) packages instant pistachio pudding	2¼	cups milk

In a mixing bowl, combine pistachio pudding and milk. Mix until thick. Pour over 1st layer.

TOPPING

1	(8-ounce) container whipped topping	½	cup finely chopped pecans

Spread whipped topping on top of second layer. Sprinkle pecans on top. Refrigerate until ready to serve.

Dewey and Karen Lofton

"If you want to make this recipe a little more healthy, fat-free or sugar-free cream cheese, whipped topping and pudding may be used."

– Karen and Dewey

174

GARDEN PENNE MEDLEY

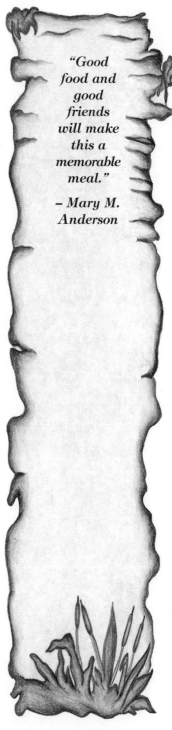

5	tablespoons olive oil
1	large purple onion, wedged
1	small green bell pepper, thinly sliced
3	yellow squash, thinly sliced
2	zucchini, thinly sliced
1	(2.25-ounce) can sliced black olives, drained
1	(8-ounce) can sliced mushrooms, drained
1-2	cloves garlic, chopped
1	(14½-ounce) can puréed Italian tomatoes
¼	teaspoon granulated sugar
	Salt and pepper
1	(8-ounce) package penne pasta, cooked
	Grated Romano cheese
	Fresh basil

Using a wok or skillet, heat olive oil. Add onions, bell peppers, squash and zucchini. Cover and simmer over low to medium heat until tender but not limp. Add black olives, mushrooms, garlic, tomatoes and sugar. Salt and pepper to taste. Cook uncovered 15 to 20 minutes. Add pasta. Cook another 5 minutes. Sprinkle Romano cheese and basil on top.

Lauralyn Maranto

"Good food and good friends will make this a memorable meal."

– Mary M. Anderson

WESTERN SHRIMP SUPREME

1 cup sliced fresh mushrooms or 1 (4½-ounce) can sliced mushroom
2 tablespoons butter
2 tablespoons all-purpose flour
½ cup light cream
1 (10¾-ounce) can condensed cream of mushroom soup
⅓ cup white wine
3 tablespoons grated Parmesan cheese
2 (10-ounce) packages large cooked and peeled shrimp
1 (16-ounce) can artichoke hearts, drained and cut in quarters
¼ cup toasted, slivered almonds
6 frozen patty shells, thawed and heated

In a skillet, cook mushrooms in butter until tender. Pour into a mixing bowl. Add flour and gradually stir in cream. Bring mixture to a boil. Cook 1 minute. Stir constantly. Blend in cream of mushroom soup, wine and Parmesan cheese. Add shrimp and artichokes. Heat thoroughly while stirring. Sprinkle almonds on top. Serve in patty shells.

Serves 6 people

Charles McClendon

PARTY CRACKER CLUTTER

1	box cheese crackers	1	tablespoon dry dill or
1	box oyster crackers		lemon pepper
½	cup olive or vegetable		seasoning, divided
	oil	2	packages ranch salad
1	tablespoon granulated		dressing mix, divided
	garlic, divided		

Place all crackers in large mixing bowl. Drizzle oil over crackers and stir until all crackers are glossy. Sprinkle half of remaining dry ingredients on top of crackers. Stir well. Repeat this step with remaining dry ingredients. Stir well. Leave crackers in bowl, stirring occasionally until all crackers are dry. Store in any airtight container.

Doris McCoin

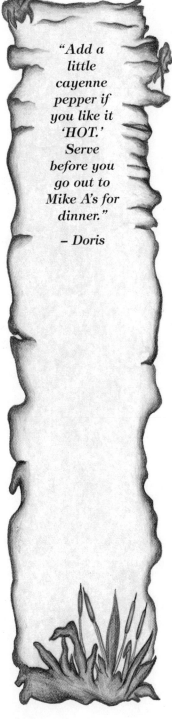

"Add a little cayenne pepper if you like it 'HOT.' Serve before you go out to Mike A's for dinner."

– Doris

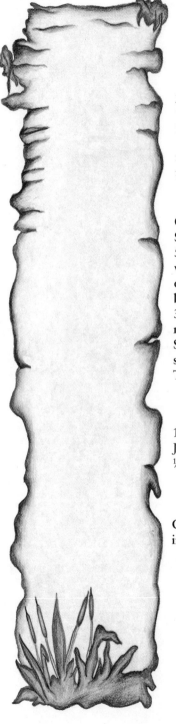

LOUISIANA CRAB CAKES

1	bunch green onions	2	teaspoons tarragon,
1	red bell pepper,		chopped
	chopped		Cavender's Greek
2	celery stalks, chopped		seasoning to taste
1	stick butter	2	cups Italian bread
1	pound white crabmeat		crumbs, divided
	(lump)	2	eggs, beaten
½	cup mayonnaise		Vegetable oil
½	cup Dijon-style		
	mustard		

Chop green onions, keeping tops and bottoms separate. Sauté bell pepper, celery and green onion bottoms in butter 5 to 7 minutes. Place crabmeat in a large bowl. Add sautéed vegetables. Fold in mayonnaise and mustard. Add green onion tops, tarragon and Cavender's Greek Seasoning. Add bread crumbs to desired consistency. Form mixture into 3-inch cakes. Dip each cake in beaten eggs and roll in remaining bread crumbs. Place in refrigerator until firm. Sauté crab cakes in vegetable oil 4 to 5 minutes on each side or until brown. Serve warm with Roasted Pepper-Caper Tartar Sauce.

ROASTED PEPPER-CAPER TARTAR SAUCE

1	cup mayonnaise	½	medium purple onion,
	Juice of 2 lemons		finely chopped
½	cup chopped roasted	¾	cup capers, drained
	red peppers	½	cup chopped parsley
			Creole seasoning to taste

Combine all ingredients and refrigerate overnight to intensify flavors.

Mary Ann Monsour

SEVEN LAYER ITALIAN DIP

1 (8-ounce) package cream cheese	⅓ cup roasted red peppers, drained
½ cup feta cheese	¼ cup chopped green onions
6 tablespoons butter	
1 tablespoon Italian seasoning	⅓ cup kalamata olives, drained
1 cup shredded Parmesan cheese, divided	1 (16-ounce) jar marinated artichoke hearts, drained
1 cup vegetable antipasto or caponata, divided	Nonstick cooking spray

Combine cream cheese, feta cheese, butter and dried Italian seasoning in food processor. Process until smooth. Set aside. Spray a 4-cup straight-sided mold, bowl or container with nonstick cooking spray. Line with plastic wrap. Layer ingredients in the following order: ½ cup Parmesan cheese, ½ cup antipasto, 1 cup cream cheese mixture, roasted red peppers, green onions, olives, artichoke hearts, ½ cup antipasto, 1 cup cream cheese mixture and ½ cup Parmesan cheese. Fold plastic over the top, press gently to compact the layers. Chill until firm. Unmold and serve with gourmet crackers or toasted bread.

Mary Ann Monsour

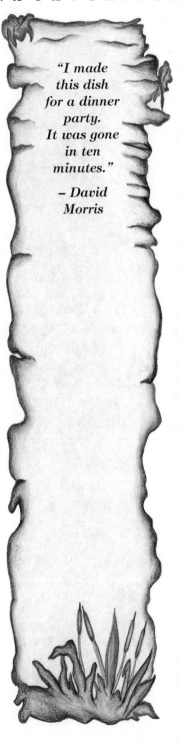

"I made this dish for a dinner party. It was gone in ten minutes."

– David Morris

SOUTH OF THE BORDER SOUTH LOUISIANA CHILI

"I love shredded cheddar cheese and crackers with mine. Also goes great over rice with a piece of Mexican cornbread. Great after hurricane season when the weather starts cooling down."

– David

"David's chili will make your eyes water and your nose run it's so spicy."

– Mary M. Anderson

4	pounds lean ground beef	
4	yellow onions, chopped	
1	green bell pepper, chopped	
2	tablespoons fresh chopped garlic	
2	medium jalapeño peppers, sliced	
2	(10-ounce) cans diced Rotel tomatoes	

2 teaspoons black pepper
2 teaspoons salt
8 teaspoons chili powder
2 packets chili seasoning mix
1 teaspoon cumin
1 (10¾-ounce) can condensed cream of mushroom soup

In a medium saucepan, brown ground beef. Strain through colander to remove excess oil. Add beef and remainder of ingredients to a large pot. Cook over medium heat until boiling. Reduce heat and simmer 45 minutes or more.

Serves 6 to 8 people

David Miller Morris, General Manager

BROTHER'S SWISS STEAK

1 (2-3 pound) round steak, quartered
1 large yellow onion, chopped
1 large green bell pepper, chopped
2 (14½-ounce) cans stewed tomatoes

2 tablespoons salt
1 tablespoon black pepper
1 tablespoon granulated sugar
4 cups water

In a large cast iron pot, combine all ingredients. Cover and cook 2 hours over medium heat. Simmer over low heat until ready to serve. Serve over rice.

Bobby Morris

GRANNY'S
CORNBREAD DRESSING

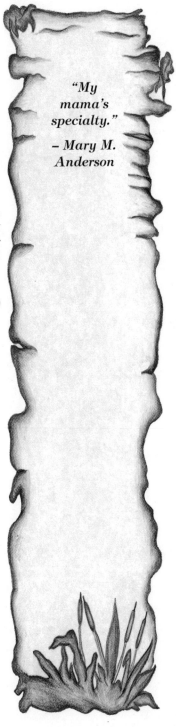

2 (8½-ounce) packages cornbread muffin mix
2 cups chopped celery
2 cups chopped yellow onions

3 cups chopped green onions
2 cups chicken or turkey broth (less for drier, more for moist)
1 tablespoon granulated sugar (optional)

"My mama's specialty."

– Mary M. Anderson

Make cornbread according to directions. In a large bowl, combine baked and crumbled cornbread, celery, yellow onions and green onions. Mix well. Add broth. Add sugar to taste if desired. Pour into a casserole dish. Cook 45 minutes to 1 hour at 375°.

Vina G. Morris (Granny)

CRAWFISH CASSEROLE

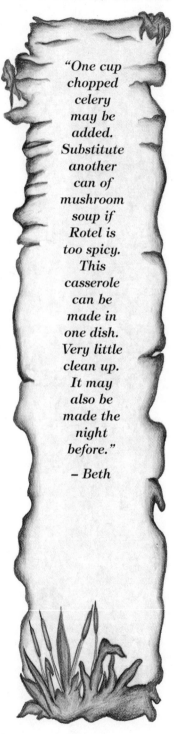

"One cup chopped celery may be added. Substitute another can of mushroom soup if Rotel is too spicy. This casserole can be made in one dish. Very little clean up. It may also be made the night before."

– Beth

1 pound crawfish tails	1 cup uncooked rice
1 (10¾-ounce) can French onion soup	¼ cup chopped green bell peppers
1 (10-ounce) can Rotel tomatoes	1 cup chopped green onions
1 (10¾-ounce) can condensed cream of mushroom soup	Salt and pepper to taste
1 stick margarine, melted	2 cups grated cheddar cheese or Monterey Jack cheese, divided

In a large greased casserole dish, combine all ingredients except cheese. Add one cup cheese. Mix well. Cover and bake 45 minutes at 350°. Uncover and sprinkle remaining 1 cup cheese on top. Bake, uncovered, 15 minutes longer. Serve.

Beth H. Perry

SWISS STEAK

2 (1-pound) round
    steaks (each ½-inch
    thick)
1½ cups flour, divided
1 teaspoon salt
1 teaspoon black pepper
1 teaspoon garlic salt
¼ cup oil
3 large yellow onions,
    sliced

3 cloves garlic, chopped
½ stalk celery, chopped
1 (6-ounce) can tomato
    paste
3-4 cups water
½-1 teaspoon granulated
    sugar
Salt and pepper

With a meat mallet, tenderize steak. In a bowl, combine 1 cup flour, salt, black pepper and garlic. Rub each side of steaks with contents of bowl. In a medium saucepan, brown each side of steaks in oil. Remove meat from saucepan and place in medium pot, reserving oil in saucepan. Cover meat with onions, garlic and celery. In saucepan where meat was browned, make a thin roux with remaining flour. Add tomato paste and roux, water and sugar. Salt and pepper to taste. Cook 1 to 1½ hours or until tender over medium to medium low heat. Serve over rice.

Louise Hitzman Petersen

"This was one dish that our family loved on a cool fall or winter night. It is a little 'heavy' to serve during the summer."

– Louise

WACKY CAKE

CAKE

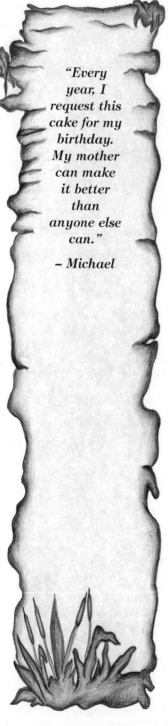

"Every year, I request this cake for my birthday. My mother can make it better than anyone else can."

– Michael

3	cups all-purpose flour, sifted	1	tablespoon vanilla extract
2	cups granulated sugar	2	tablespoons white vinegar
6	tablespoons cocoa mix	⅔	cup vegetable oil
2	teaspoons baking soda	2	cups water
1	teaspoon salt		

In a large mixing bowl, combine flour, sugar, cocoa, baking soda and salt. Mix with hands. Using your finger, make 3 holes in mixture. In first hole, pour vanilla extract. In second hole, pour vinegar, and in third hole, pour vegetable oil. Add water to bowl. Mix well. Pour mixture into an ungreased pan. Bake 40 to 45 minutes at 350°. Let cool. Top with frosting.

FROSTING

4	tablespoons butter	2	tablespoons milk
6	tablespoons brown sugar	2	tablespoons vanilla extract
¼	teaspoon salt		Powdered sugar

In a small saucepan, combine butter and brown sugar. Cook over low heat until butter is melted. Add salt, milk, vanilla extract and powdered sugar (enough to cover cake).

Michael Petersen

EASY BRISKET

2	teaspoons liquid smoke	2	teaspoons onion salt
2	teaspoons garlic salt	½	(12-ounce) can beer
		8	pounds brisket

In a mixing bowl, combine liquid smoke, garlic salt, onion salt and beer and pour over brisket. Marinate over night. Drain brisket and place in a baking dish. Cover baking dish with aluminum foil. Bake 7 hours at 300°.

Ron Petersen Sr.

CRAWFISH ÉTOUFFÉE

1	bunch green onions, finely chopped	2	cups chicken broth (or 8 cups for 5 pound tails)
4	tablespoons butter		Salt and pepper
1½	pounds crawfish tails	2	tablespoons paprika
3	tablespoons flour		Parsley

In a medium pot, sauté green onions in butter until tender. Using a colander, strain crawfish tails, reserving drained liquid. Set tails aside. Combine reserved liquid, flour and chicken broth in a saucepan. Whip until smooth. Cook 30 to 40 minutes over medium heat. Add crawfish tails, salt, pepper and paprika. Cook 30 minutes or until tender. Serve over rice and garnish with parsley.

Richard Picou, also known as "Q"

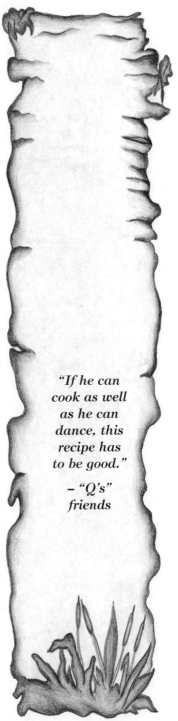

"If he can cook as well as he can dance, this recipe has to be good."

– "Q's" friends

EASY SEAFOOD GUMBO

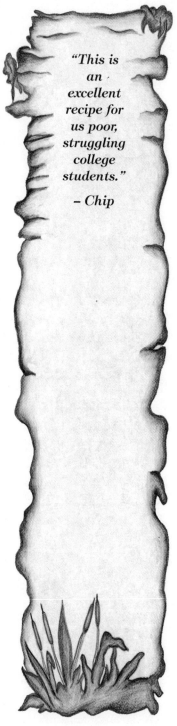

"This is an excellent recipe for us poor, struggling college students."

– Chip

½ cup oil
½ cup all-purpose flour
1 large yellow onion, finely chopped
1 large green bell pepper, finely chopped
½ cup chopped celery
1 (15-ounce) can tomato sauce

1 (7-ounce) can sliced mushrooms, drained
1 (15-ounce) can cream style corn
Salt and pepper
1 pound fresh shrimp, peeled
1 pound white crabmeat (lump or backfin)
Oysters (optional)

In a large pot, combine oil and flour to make a roux. Add onions, bell peppers and celery. Simmer until vegetables are tender. Add tomato sauce, mushrooms and corn. Bring to a rolling boil. Season to taste with salt and pepper. Simmer over low heat. Thirty minutes before serving, add seafood and simmer until done. Serve over rice.

Chip Robert

GUMBO CHOU
(FRENCH FOR CABBAGE)

1 medium chicken, cut up	½ green bell pepper, chopped
Salt	
Black pepper	2 cloves garlic, chopped
Cayenne pepper	
Vegetable oil (enough to brown chicken)	1 celery stalk, chopped
	1-1½ cups water
1 large yellow onion, chopped	1 large head cabbage, shredded

Season chicken with salt, black pepper and cayenne pepper to taste. Brown well in vegetable oil using moderate to high heat (This is the secret to the dish). Set chicken aside. Add onions, bell peppers, garlic and celery. Cover and sauté until tender. Stir frequently. Add previously set aside chicken. Add 1 to 1½ cups water. Stir to loosen gravy stock. Slowly add cabbage and let smother down. This should produce thin, golden gravy. Serve over rice.

Serves 6 to 8 people

Chip Robert

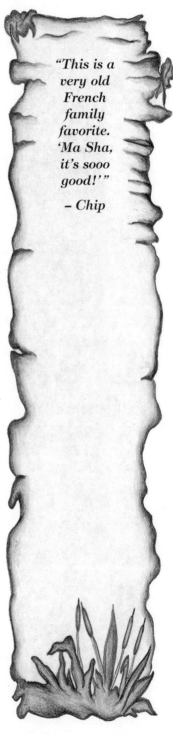

"This is a very old French family favorite. 'Ma Sha, it's sooo good!'"

– Chip

187

JAMBALAYA

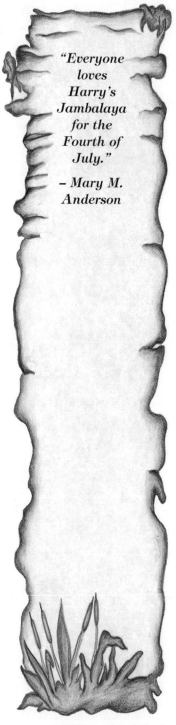

"*Everyone loves Harry's Jambalaya for the Fourth of July.*"

– Mary M. Anderson

2	skinless chicken fryers	7	cups water
½	cup vegetable oil		Salt
1	large Vidalia onion, chopped		Garlic salt
			Cayenne pepper
1	pound smoked mild "Vernon" pork sausage		Black pepper
		4	cups uncooked rice

Cut chicken into pieces. In a heavy aluminum or cast iron pot, fry chicken in vegetable oil. Season chicken as desired while frying. When chicken is done, quickly remove oil from pot and discard. Continue cooking chicken until golden brown. Allow a residue to form on bottom of pot. Remove chicken and set aside. In the same pot, sauté onions. When onions are tender, add sausage to saucepan. Simmer until onions are fully sautéed. Add water. Stir. Season to taste with salt, garlic salt, cayenne pepper and black pepper. Bring mixture to a boil. Boil 10 minutes. Reduce heat and add chicken. Bring back to a boil. Add rice. Simmer until rice is tender.

Harry Robert

MEXICAN PORK ROAST

6	red chiles or chipotle peppers, canned or dried	½	cup brown sugar
		2	cups Coke, divided
10-12	cloves garlic, divided	1	(3½-pound) pork loin roast
1	tablespoon crushed oregano		Salt and pepper
1	tablespoon crushed basil	2	tablespoons vegetable oil

If using dried chiles, boil in water and let stand until soft; drain. Remove stem, seeds and veins. Combine chiles, 6 cloves garlic, oregano, basil, brown sugar and ½ cup Coke in a food processor. Process. Season roast with salt and pepper. Make slits in roast and insert remaining garlic cloves. Rub roast in oil. Place in a baking pan. Spread chile mixture over meat. Pour remaining 1½ cups Coke on top of roast. Cover and bake 2 hours at 350°. Uncover and cook 1 hour. Let stand 15 minutes before serving.

Jeanne Robert, a.k.a. "Jean, Jean the Poboy Machine"

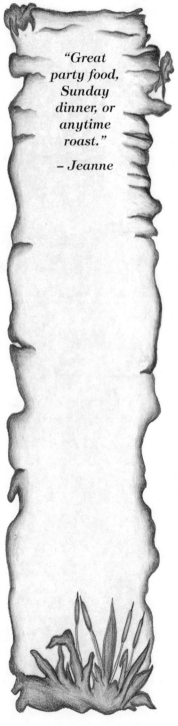

"Great party food, Sunday dinner, or anytime roast."

– Jeanne

T's TASTY SALSA

1	(10-ounce) can diced Rotel tomatoes	1	jalapeño pepper, finely chopped
2	carrots, chopped	3	tablespoons red wine vinegar
1	small purple onion, chopped	2	tablespoons hot sauce
1	small yellow onion, chopped	2	tablespoons granulated sugar
1	green bell pepper, chopped	1	tablespoon black pepper
½	bunch cilantro, chopped	1	bag tortilla chips

Chop fresh vegetables to desired size. In a medium bowl, combine all ingredients except chips. Mix well. Refrigerate and serve with tortilla chips.

Taylor Robert

MOCK OYSTER DIP

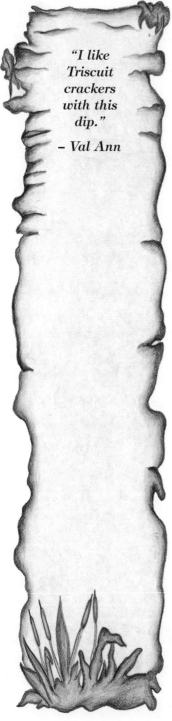

"I like Triscuit crackers with this dip."

– Val Ann

2	packages frozen chopped broccoli, thawed and drained
1	medium yellow onion, chopped
4	tablespoons butter
2	(10¾-ounce) cans condensed cream of mushroom soup
2	garlic cheese rolls
2	(4-ounce) cans sliced mushrooms, drained
½	can slivered almonds
	Salt
	Cayenne pepper

In a medium saucepan, sauté broccoli and onions in butter. Cook over low heat until tender. Stir frequently. Set aside. In a double boiler, add mushroom soup, garlic cheese rolls and sliced mushrooms. Heat until smooth. Pour in large bowl. Add broccoli mixture and almonds. Stir well. Add salt and cayenne pepper to taste.

Val Ann Robert

WESLEY ROBERT'S PEANUT BRITTLE

3	cups granulated sugar
1¼	cups light corn syrup
⅔	cup water
3	cups raw peanuts
¼	teaspoon salt
1	tablespoon baking soda

In a large pot, combine sugar, corn syrup, water, peanuts and salt. Bring mixture to a boil. Let boil until candy thermometer reaches 315°. Remove from heat. Quickly add soda. Stir using a wooden spoon. Pour into a greased baking pan. Mixture will spread on its own. Let cool. Break with a knife. Store in air-tight containers.

Wesley Robert

JAMBALAYA

1   (10-ounce) bag
      Seasoning Blend
      (onion, celery, bell
      peppers and parsley)
2   tablespoons butter
1   heaping teaspoon
      minced garlic
Smoked sausage

Smoked turkey
1   (10-ounce) can diced
      Rotel tomatoes
1   (8-ounce) can tomato
      sauce
2   cups uncooked rice
2½   cups water
Salt and pepper

In a heavy pot, sauté Seasoning Blend in butter. Add garlic
and desired amount of sausage and turkey. Add Rotel
tomatoes, tomato sauce, rice and water. Bring mixture to a
boil. Reduce heat to medium. Cover and stir occasionally.
Salt and pepper to taste. Cook 30 to 40 minutes. Remove
from heat while still moist.

Serves 6 to 8 people

Al and Patricia Rodrigue

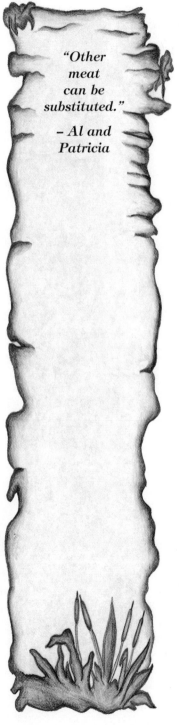

*"Other
meat
can be
substituted."*

*– Al and
Patricia*

U.S. OPEN DUCK

Take two green-headed mallards, preferably killed by Mike
himself. Cut duck in quarters and brown in oil in a cast
iron pot. Salt and pepper the duck to taste while browning.
Add as much cayenne pepper as you like. Remove the duck
from pot and make a dark brown roux by adding flour to
the pot. Next add onions, bell peppers, garlic and chopped
green onions. As it cooks, add water to help soften the
mix. When the vegetables are cooked, add duck. Cover
with water. Simmer 3 to 4 hours. Serve the duck over rice
with cranberry sauce. Eating this dish is almost as enjoyable
as the U.S. Open.

Dr. Gayle Sanchez

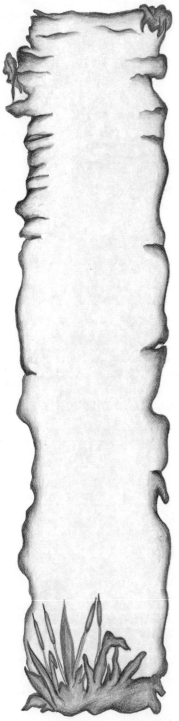

CORN BEEF DIP

1 (12-ounce) can corn beef	2 tablespoons parsley flakes
2 cups sour cream	2 teaspoons Accent or Bon Appetit seasoning
2 cups mayonnaise	
2 teaspoons dill seed	
2 tablespoons chopped green onions	2 loaves rye bread, divided

In a large bowl, combine all ingredients except bread. Mix well. Using 1 loaf of bread, hollow out a bowl shape. Use for serving dip. Slice second loaf and use for dipping.

Mary P. Sandoval

WALT'S JUICY GRILLED STEAKS

1 stick butter	4-6 (1½-inch thick) beef tenderloin steaks
6 tablespoons Moore's Marinade or favorite marinade	

In a small saucepan, melt butter and add marinade. Season steaks as you prefer. Dredge seasoned steaks through sauce. Place on a very hot grill. Sear one minute on each side. Dredge steak again through sauce. Grill steaks 3 to 4 minutes on each side for medium rare.

Serves 4 to 6 people

Lucy and Jimmie Walters

I•N•D•E•X

C

P

PASTA

PORK

POTATOES

"Recipes From Mike Anderson's Seafood Restaurant and Other South Louisiana Favorites"

Please send me _____ copies of "Recipes
From Mike Anderson's Seafood Restaurant
and Other South Louisiana Favorites"   @ $18.95 each   _____

Mike Anderson's South Louisiana Seasoning   @ $ 2.50 each   _____

Shipping and Handling for the 1st book   @ $ 3.75   _____

Shipping and Handling for 1st MAS Seasoning   @ $ 3.50   _____

Shipping and Handling
for each additional book/Seasoning   @ $ 2.50 each   _____

Louisiana (Residents Only) State Tax   @   9% each   _____

    NO CHECKS   Total $ _____

**Money Order enclosed made payable to Mike Anderson's Seafood Restaurant
Attn: Cookbook, 1031 West Lee Drive, Baton Rouge, LA 70820**

Name_____

Address_____

City_____ State_____ Zip Code_____

Telephone Number (_____)_____

Please charge to my   ☐ MasterCard   ☐ VISA   ☐ American Express

Card #_____ Expiration Date_____

Signature of Card holder_____

Or order by phone: 1-800-899-8428

- -

"Recipes From Mike Anderson's Seafood Restaurant and Other South Louisiana Favorites"

Please send me _____ copies of "Recipes
From Mike Anderson's Seafood Restaurant
and Other South Louisiana Favorites"   @ $18.95 each   _____

Mike Anderson's South Louisiana Seasoning   @ $ 2.50 each   _____

Shipping and Handling for the 1st book   @ $ 3.75   _____

Shipping and Handling for 1st MAS Seasoning   @ $ 3.50   _____

Shipping and Handling
for each additional book/Seasoning   @ $ 2.50 each   _____

Louisiana (Residents Only) State Tax   @   9% each   _____

    NO CHECKS   Total $ _____

**Money Order enclosed made payable to Mike Anderson's Seafood Restaurant
Attn: Cookbook, 1031 West Lee Drive, Baton Rouge, LA 70820**

Name_____

Address_____

City_____ State_____ Zip Code_____

Telephone Number (_____)_____

Please charge to my   ☐ MasterCard   ☐ VISA   ☐ American Express

Card #_____ Expiration Date_____

Signature of Card holder_____

Or order by phone: 1-800-899-8428

"Recipes From Mike Anderson's Seafood Restaurant and Other South Louisiana Favorites"

Please send me _____ copies of "Recipes
    From Mike Anderson's Seafood Restaurant
    and Other South Louisiana Favorites"   @ $18.95 each   _____

Mike Anderson's South Louisiana Seasoning   @ $ 2.50 each   _____

Shipping and Handling for the 1st book   @ $ 3.75   _____

Shipping and Handling for 1st MAS Seasoning   @ $ 3.50   _____

Shipping and Handling
    for each additional book/Seasoning   @ $ 2.50 each   _____

Louisiana (Residents Only) State Tax   @   9% each   _____

    NO CHECKS   Total $ _____

**Money Order enclosed made payable to Mike Anderson's Seafood Restaurant
Attn: Cookbook, 1031 West Lee Drive, Baton Rouge, LA 70820**

Name_____

Address_____

City_____ State_____ Zip Code_____

Telephone Number (_____)_____

Please charge to my   ☐ MasterCard   ☐ VISA   ☐ American Express

Card #_____ Expiration Date_____

Signature of Card holder_____

Or order by phone: 1-800-899-8428

"Recipes From Mike Anderson's Seafood Restaurant and Other South Louisiana Favorites"

Please send me _____ copies of "Recipes
    From Mike Anderson's Seafood Restaurant
    and Other South Louisiana Favorites"   @ $18.95 each   _____

Mike Anderson's South Louisiana Seasoning   @ $ 2.50 each   _____

Shipping and Handling for the 1st book   @ $ 3.75   _____

Shipping and Handling for 1st MAS Seasoning   @ $ 3.50   _____

Shipping and Handling
    for each additional book/Seasoning   @ $ 2.50 each   _____

Louisiana (Residents Only) State Tax   @   9% each   _____

    NO CHECKS   Total $ _____

**Money Order enclosed made payable to Mike Anderson's Seafood Restaurant
Attn: Cookbook, 1031 West Lee Drive, Baton Rouge, LA 70820**

Name_____

Address_____

City_____ State_____ Zip Code_____

Telephone Number (_____)_____

Please charge to my   ☐ MasterCard   ☐ VISA   ☐ American Express

Card #_____ Expiration Date_____

Signature of Card holder_____

Or order by phone: 1-800-899-8428